Ghostly North Carolina

Ghostly North Carolina

Hauntings from Mountains to Coast

James M. Parker

Exposit

Jefferson, North Carolina

Unless otherwise noted, all photographs are by the author.

LIBRARY OF CONGRESS CATALOGUING-IN-PUBLICATION DATA

Names: Parker, James M., 1997– author.
Title: Ghostly North Carolina : hauntings from mountains to coast / James M. Parker.
Description: Jefferson, North Carolina : Exposit, 2024. | Includes index.
Identifiers: LCCN 2024004588 | ISBN 9781476694771 (paperback : acid free paper) ∞
ISBN 9781476652108 (ebook)
Subjects: LCSH: Haunted places—North Carolina. | Ghosts—North Carolina. |
BISAC: BODY, MIND & SPIRIT / Parapsychology / ESP (Clairvoyance,
Precognition, Telepathy) | BODY, MIND & SPIRIT / Parapsychology / General
Classification: LCC BF1472.U6 P367 2024 | DDC 133.109756—dc23/eng/20240213
LC record available at https://lccn.loc.gov/2024004588

BRITISH LIBRARY CATALOGUING DATA ARE AVAILABLE

ISBN (print) 978-1-4766-9477-1
ISBN (ebook) 978-1-4766-5210-8

Front cover image: © Savvapanf Photo/Shutterstock

———

Printed in the United States of America

Exposit is an imprint of McFarland & Company, Inc., Publishers

Exposit
Box 611, Jefferson, North Carolina 28640
www.expositbooks.com

To my wife and children who, together with me, ventured past the point of sanity to meet the lifeless inhabitants residing in each of these chilling locations; my father who first introduced me to the world of the paranormal and has since joined said world; my mentor, Robert Pohle, without his guidance, this book would have remained nothing more than a reoccurring nightmare in my mind; to Sara Karloff, who enjoyed these true stories so much that she agreed to endorse it; lastly, I dedicate this book to the ghosts you are about to meet. May their memories live on as they haunt your nightmares...

Table of Contents

Introduction

The ghosts are moving at present. Restless; beckoning your attention. May I introduce myself? I'm James Parker. I will be your host as you read and explore the most haunted and paranormally active locations in all of North Carolina. In a way, consider this book a written tour; a blood-curdling adventure through North Carolina's haunted reality. The "Old North State" stands as one of the most unique and diverse places in America. In virtually all ways, from its mountainous regions, valleys and hollows, to its pristine beaches and coastal communities, it seems to fit all definitions of "the perfect State." Geographical differences are not the only factors which give North Carolina its well-rounded character. Nestled within each portion of the state's almost opposing natural wonders, are people and cities mimicking their surroundings. All the way from the mountain folk wearing hand-patched clothes, speaking a peculiar, Appalachian dialect, to the bleached-hair and sun-kissed skin of the "beach bum" who gives the illusion of being in California, from one end of North Carolina to the other, it's difficult to remember, it's all the same state.

In a way, this book is just that, a tour, introducing you to some of the state's locals who seem to have never left ... even after death. However, in another way, it is something much bigger. If I may be so bold to say, you are in for a treat. The majority of these accounts have yet to be made public. Not only does the publication of this book serve as "bits of true horror" to fuel your nightmares, but it also stands as the debut of much of North Carolina's authentic hauntings. I'll be honest. When pondering the idea of this collection of bone-chilling encounters, I wanted this to be different from anything else available which you might use

1

to curb your hunger for darkness. I wish to bring you something more tangible.

I did not want to waste paper and ink rewriting (for the thousandth time) the traditional "folk lore" passed to each new generation from the previous. Rather, I considered two fundamental aspects for this book: the tangibility of each story and that each account be true. They are places you may visit, if your courage allows (and if you're crazy enough). The people mentioned within these haunted pages are real people who, when agreeing to have their names and experiences eternally etched within this collection, agree also to share their personal encounters, in their own words, on a one-on-one basis. Throughout this collection, you'll encounter the voices of the dead lurking near heavily populated areas, apparitions of lifeless beings terrorizing rural communities, and much more. Who knows, perhaps some of these lost souls reside in your own back yard... Each haunt is brought to life through a unique integration of traditional storytelling techniques with journalist and first-hand accounts.

One of the most terrifying facts about this book, other than each account being true, is the fact that each location, though prominent, are everyday areas. Perhaps, as you read through these pages (which I don't suggest you do alone) you'll come across an eatery you frequent, perhaps the local cinema or theater, or even that school or cemetery which gives you a *weird feeling* as you pass it on your daily commute. Don't forget the bridge you cross over before passing the school or graveyard; we'll discuss what hides beneath it as well. Maybe, at the completion of this book, you'll finally be able to explain that *thing* that happened to you when you visited that spot, or ate at that restaurant, or drove by that cemetery. Maybe, just maybe, you'll be able to put a name to that face you saw watching you as you walked past that old, brick, two-story building.

I am proud to say that I am the first to interview many of the *special guests* you'll soon meet on this chilling tour. This book is the first record, exposing the poltergeists and trapped souls which, knowingly or unknowingly, surround you. This collection of never-before-heard, true ghost stories are not based upon local legends or faraway places. Rather, they are factors which exist in reality, just as you and I; a reality which you and I know like the back of our hands. Yes, this collection of encounters with beings from beyond the grave is a treat indeed, for it is unlike any other.

About the Research

I had the privilege of majoring in psychology at Regent University. In like manner, I am certified in historical studies through Harvard University. Throughout the research process, I relied upon each of these disciplines to ensure the authenticity and accuracy of the information I present. I combined these learned skills with the, what seems like, biological interest and connection to all things "spooky." My parents were a pair of television horror hosts based in Berks County, Pennsylvania. Perhaps the odd draw to the darker side of life is hereditary...

Nevertheless, some of these locations were presented to me as potential paranormal hotspots (Revival 1869) whilst others earned their place in this collection once I found enough historical data pointing to a potential haunting and mustered enough courage to reach out by means of cold-calling (The Howell Theater). Once a successful lead was in place, I conducted various interviews with each person claiming to have experienced a paranormal phenomenon. Naturally, I utilized my knowledge in psychology to rule out any lurking variables pertaining to the recollections conveyed to me that might cause the account to be dismissible. In other words, each quotation you'll read and each piece of interview your soon-to-be terrified eyes will gaze upon in this book remains unexplainable according to the scientific perspective. In like manner, each fact told to me has been double, no, triple, not that either, quad–, well, you get the point. Each historical variable held between the pages of this book has been checked not only by me, a life-long student of history, but other credible sources as well. But enough with the academic endeavors linked to these accounts. Let's talk about something even more interesting, something which caused you to pick up this book in the first place: fear.

Live in Fear
for

You're driving on the interstate. You've turned the volume on the radio so low it might as well be off. Your clammy palms grip the ten and two o'clock positions on the steering wheel like a tween undergoing a dreaded driving test. Though nearly silenced, your ears pick up the few distinct opening notes of your favorite song that just came on the radio; you haven't heard it in months. Yet, your nervous hands remain glued to the wheel. Why? Because the three or four pairs of blinking hazard lights in front of you are the only things visible through the fogged windshield due to the aggressive, torrential downpour. It's raining. Not just a normal rain, the water pelts your car and highway at such an unprecedented speed that you fear crossing the bridge suspended over the small creek thinking the moment you reach the bridge's midway, an unannounced current is going to swift you over the bridge, never to be seen again.

Even with this fear, you do not allow your fixed eyes to glance at the bridge's side. Thirty seconds after you cross the bridge, a new set of lights emerge from the haze created by the tropical rain. These lights are a different shade. The vehicle appears to have more lights than the pairs of two you've been staring at. You notice that, unlike the other hazard lights, these lights are not moving and blink rapidly. As you arrive closer, you realize that the stationary lights belong to an ambulance. In front of the ambulance is a car that looks as if an F-5 tornado had just spit it out after carrying it about fifty miles. The car flipped. Directly next to the destroyed car is a white sheet-like structure. "I wonder if there's a body under that sheet," you ask yourself. Perhaps even ask whoever is in the car with you. A honk breaks your concentration from the scene. You jerk your head back to the road. Lucky for you, you manage to swerve back into your own lane after unconsciously glancing to your left, searching for a dead body left over from the car wreck.

I find it increasingly interesting that we crave fear. Humanity, in a way, lives to be afraid. Deep within the human psyche is the attraction to the strange, dark, and mysterious. Some might even call the attraction a sick obsession; perhaps it is. Whatever the case may be, we remain attracted to that which we fear. Even if we abhor it, something deep within us is drawn to it. Logically, we wouldn't dare attempt to "sneak a peek" at a recently killed human. Especially someone who had just met his or her gruesome end by means of a car crash. Perhaps, when we judge others rubbernecking as they pass the dramatic, distasteful scene taking place on the side of the highway, we say to ourselves—perhaps even to our passenger—how shameful it is that people somehow find interest in such heart-breaking tragedies. We might even give a small speech to our unattentive passengers on how wrong it is to be so nosey (especially when something so horrific had just taken place). I mean, it doesn't concern us, wouldn't you agree? Yet, when we find ourselves given the opportunity to glance in the face of fear, we take it. Often, without giving a single thought.

Why is that? Why do we crave that uncomfortable feeling? What is it, hiding deep within the shadows of the human mind, which finds a morbid sense of satisfaction over that which disturbs us? There are countless theories which might explain the thought provoking question. One might be offered from the perspective of evolutionary psychology. When fear stimuli are presented, the human mind releases chemicals such as epinephrine and adrenaline. These hormones, which shoot throughout the body, also mix with dopamine, causing a sort of euphoric experience. The thought is, our ancestors were able to become "superhuman" when these fear stimulated hormones were released, and thus, having the ability to escape any danger presented. Now, they serve as targets which masters of entertainment trigger. In other words, humans enjoy the "fight or flight" state. It adds a sense of thrill to life. At least, that's the psychological understanding as to why we are attracted to fear.

Though this may be true, I believe there is something deeper, perhaps even mystical, which contributes to why we are attracted to things from which, logically, we should look away. Why are we so interested in death? Perhaps the opposite can also be asked, why are we so afraid of it? We all must shake hands with it one day! Why are we so fascinated by horror? What about the paranormal piques our interests? Is it that we wish to know what happens after death? Maybe, seeing a ghost will vanquish any doubts we have created. I would be a fool if I claimed to have the answers to all the questions I've asked. The truth is, I don't know. I don't know why I crave fear; I don't know why I love (and I mean *love*) to get scared; I don't know why I try to look under the dignity-protecting white sheet thrown up on the side of the interstate. I do know, however, that I love the macabre interests; I love the sweaty palms dangling by my sides as I approach a haunted location; I love hearing a distinct voice whispering, "Get out." Directly behind me and, when I look, there's no one there; most of all, I've loved getting to know the haunts within this book. My wish for you, dear reader, is that you come to love them too. Who knows, perhaps one of *them* will grow to love you...

Happy Haunts,
J.M. Parker

Class Is in Session

Asheville, Buncombe County

"Time for school!" A phrase all too familiar to anyone past the age of five. To some, it is nothing more than a normal occurrence, "a part of life," if you will, and arouses feelings of excitement, discipline, and dedication—albeit, on rare occasions. To others, well, let's face it, to most, the call to school is received in similar fashion as one receiving the ultimate death sentence, ushering feelings of dread and great annoyance. Ah, yes, good times (some might say). As adults look back at their "school days" the nostalgic memories are expressed by one of the two following phrases, "I sure do miss those days!" Or, "I'm glad that's over!" Whatever the relationship between yourself and school may be, the either cherished or hated sound off, "Time for school" never conjures up feelings of being haunted ... that is, unless you graduated from Clyde A. Erwin High School.

Better known as Erwin High School, this educational institution is nestled in perhaps the most visited city of North Carolina's mountains, Asheville. Built between 1974 and 1975, the school itself resembles the design of almost any other school. Constructed of the traditional brick and mortar used for virtually every other government-funded building in the nation, dressed in a classic gray paint with a lighter, almost white trim around the top of the building. The words "CLYDE A. ERWIN HIGH SCHOOL" are placed high, capable of being seen from miles away. Each letter coated in red, stands out like the light from a lighthouse. The only difference regarding this school's appearance is that it is nestled in the mountains. Most schools have fields or forests, perhaps a road running in front of it, Erwin's scenic views are large, towering mountains; each peak lightly hazed with that magical blue fog which gives

11

these mountains the name "Blue Ridge." Yet, there is another attribute calling for attention from this school. Another attribute that transforms this average North Carolina high school into a child's—or any adult's—worst nightmare.

A school was not the original intent for the grounds on which the institution was built. In fact, a school was never part of the plan. The grounds were first sectioned off to be used as a place to store the dead, a cemetery. The "County Home Cemetery," which was founded in the early 1800s, served as the resting grounds for the poor and elderly who had no family to claim their deceased bodies, and perhaps others whose identities remained unknown. Perhaps a more fitting name for this cemetery would have been "Cemetery for the Forgotten." Nevertheless, this was the intent, and active use, for the grounds on which now stands Erwin High School. Local oral tradition states that the graves were dug by inexperienced gravediggers. Therefore, they were not the classical six-feet-down as is law when a body is entombed. Far from it, the graves were so shallow that, by the early 1940s, cemetery caretakers found skulls and other bones protruding from the ground. Over time, the skulls and whatever other human remains which decided to resurface were collected and re-buried together in a single, new grave.

By the disturbing end of the cemetery's life, the grounds were home to a thousand decaying corpses. During the early months of the year 1973, the local school administrative system sought to begin plans for building a separate location specifically for the high school. Previously, both the middle and high school classes were combined in one location. The school board controversially decided to use the County Cemetery as the location for Buncombe County's newest school. The decision was met with heated debates and much disapproval, as this move would prohibit the dead from resting in peace. Despite the backlash, the relocation of the graves began.

However, there exists a rather dark and disturbing truth regarding relocating the poorly dug graves. Since the cemetery stood as a place to bury those forgotten, perhaps unknown, there was only one headstone which indicated that the surrounding grounds were filled with the dead. Thus, most of the thousand resting bodies remained unmarked. Another, more disturbing, factor remained to be unearthed. In the early days of mountain burials, bodies were placed in wooden coffins which were then lowered into the darkness of the ground. Boards of wood were then placed across the handmade coffins in hopes of creating a barrier between the coffin's lid and the weight of the soil. Over time, like the body, the planks of wood which lay across the coffin gave, allowing the heavy dirt to crash upon (and even into) the coffin. This not only sped the process of decay but allowed the wood, both from the planks and the coffin, to return to nothingness.

These variables were realized when the mass exhumation commenced. It was impossible to locate every grave and some graves were unable to be relocated due to the poor state of the coffins and bodies. After the unprecedented exhumation was completed, a total of roughly six hundred graves were relocated, leaving hundreds of zombie-like bodies to call Erwin High School their new home.

The Hauntings at Erwin

After the majority of graves were relocated to the new County Home Cemetery, the heat and disapproval seemed to lessen. Naturally, there still remains—even to this day—select individuals who remember the outrageous move with great disappointment. Though six hundred bodies were saved, countless bodies remain underneath the halls and classrooms of Erwin High School. Difficult to comprehend, isn't it? A rotten corpse lying beneath a student's chair as he or she studies algebra. I digress. Not soon after school was in session, strange and unexplainable things began to happen to both students and faculty.

Pay Attention to Lectures; Not *Me*

A science class was in full swing. The teacher was engaging with his students and the students with their teacher. There was a mid-term exam coming up. In other words, crunch time for the students. The teacher chose to lecture on the properties of natural gasses. He prepared notes which he placed on the warm, thick glass screen of the school's projector. He began by defining and explaining oxygen. After oxygen, he naturally segued into carbon dioxide; then nitrogen; then helium and so forth. The class seemed to be losing steam. It was towards the end of the session, it was the last class for the day, and he knew other teachers had been hounding these poor children in last minute attempts to prepare them for exam week.

"How can I make this more interesting to teenagers?" the teacher asked himself between spelling out scientific phrases and theories on the white board. He paused for a moment as he turned from staring at the bright light of the projector glass to the white board which remained in the darkened room, out of the way of the projector's beam. He took a moment for his eyes to adjust to the extreme differences in light. As he paused, students took the opportunity to catch up on their notes. The teacher pondered how he might introduce an interesting topic to the conversation.

"Let's discuss the gasses released during the decomposition process." The teacher blurted out once he arrived at a stopping point in his prearranged notes. The slight chatters from disengaged students quieted, he knew he had obtained their attention once again. "Given the history of this school, I thought it would be a fun topic to discuss the lesser-known gasses. Who knows, questions pertaining to this topic might be extra credit on the exam! Can anyone tell me what gas is released during the decomposition process?"

"Ammonia and methane," one student casually says from the back of the room. "Very good," the teacher responds as he tries to hide the puzzled look on his face. He didn't expect anyone to know the answer. The teacher continues in his oddly satisfying talk on the putrefaction process. When another question is asked,

"Are there really bodies under the school?" a voice calls out from the crowd of younger eyes staring at the teacher. "Let's remember to raise our hands when we have questions," the teacher kindly reminds the class, "But, yes. The school is built on the old County Home Cemetery plot."

14

"Were the bodies removed?" another student queries. "Well, yes, but not all of them. You see, it's very diffic–."

"Are there any ghosts in the school?" another voice questions from the sea of teenagers. Annoyed, the teacher pauses to silently scold the inquirer before answering in a sharp tone. "I don't think so. I've been here for five years and have never seen anything paranormal."

"That doesn't mean ghosts aren't here," a voice proclaimed from the corner section of the gallery. "You're right. But it would be rather impossible to examine the topic from the scientific perspective. Science is the study of the natural world; things observable; measurable things." The teacher continued explaining why he doesn't believe in the paranormal as the Q&A session quickly slid into a debate over the existence of the paranormal. In an attempt to settle the debate the teacher said, "I can assure you all that there will be no questions as to the existence of ghosts and ghouls on the exam. I suggest you return back to your stud—." "CRASH!"

His last speech for the class was disrupted yet again. This time, not by a curious teenage student. The projector which still projected images of gas particles and their cycles onto the wall forcefully slid from the table on which it sat and plummeted to the ground with a jolting slam, causing the glass to shatter. The teacher did not speak a word, nor did the students move a muscle. No one was near the projector at the time of its movement. It became very clear in that moment that something, or *someone,* aggressively forced the projector to the ground. It appears that *someone* did not wish to be the center of attention and decided to end the debate once and for all.

Janitor's Night Shift

Janitors and school cleaning crews have some of the toughest jobs. Cleaning up after children (both small and overgrown) who seem to have never been taught to clean up after themselves and care for things that do not belong to them is hard work. They also receive very little-if-any gratitude for their work. Even tougher I might add, are the janitorial duties of those employed at Erwin

High School. For the tasks presented to these maintenance employees, one must *be* tough. It is not totally uncommon for janitors to stay after hours, sometimes even during the night hours, preparing the school for operations or conducting tasks which present themselves as impossible whilst the hallways and classrooms are filled with people. Our next bone-chilling encounter takes place in this very setting. After hours during the night, alone, in the echoing hallways and abandoned classrooms of the Erwin High School.

Our main character: one of the veteran janitors employed by Erwin High School. Though names will not be used in this recollection, both the janitorial team as well as myself invite you to ask any janitor at the high school about the otherworldly accounts shared amongst themselves when no one is around ... at least, no *living* person is around. Shall we continue?

"The night began as any other night I've had to work the night shift. We work at night when we need to coat the floors with wax or repair larger sections of the school or when we need to do anything else that would be difficult with people passing through," states one of the Erwin staff members. "This particular night, I was conducting a detailed clean of the hallways and rooms." He entered the school around five in the afternoon and didn't leave the premises until ten at night. Pulling into the school's parking lot, he noticed the lack of any teachers' cars. Sometimes, teachers will stay longer after school lets out to work on lesson plans, grading, and whatever other school related tasks they may need to finish. The absence of cars was a good sign for our friend. This meant that the school was completely empty, which meant he would be able to complete his task without having to stop to "shoot the breeze" with a teacher and waste precious time he could have spent cleaning.

Unlocking the side entrance door, he entered the school and began his prep work. "No time like the present." He sighed under his breath as he loaded his large, rolling gray trash can filled with cleaning supplies. A bright yellow cloth resembling Batman's utility belt was fashioned around the can filled with sprays and smaller cleaning tools. The janitor rolled the trash can deeper into the isolated section of the school. "I'll start at the back of the school and work my way to the front." He planned to himself as he walked. Each footstep echoed on the walls on either side of him; each time he stepped with his left foot, the keychain on that hip jingled its all too familiar sound.

"Hello?" The janitor threw the greeting/question into the silent air as he halted his stroll and turned around. A faint humming came from about ten feet directly behind him. The humming was so audible and unmistakable that he left his wagon to investigate. "Maybe I missed a car on my way in." He thought as he checked the three classrooms adjacent each side of him. There was no one inside nor was there a sign of any current occupants. Before he had the chance to peel his vision from glancing into the darkened third classroom, a deep roar began to fill the hall. "What in the world!" He instinctively shouted as he yanked his head in the direction of the sound. His wagon was moving, rolling quickly only to slowly come to a complete stop as if someone had pushed it. One eyebrow lifted as he scratched his beard. No one was in the hallway other than him—or so he thought.

"Grabbing my trash can, I continued on my way. I thought it was a little weird that I heard someone humming behind me, then my wagon started rolling by itself." The janitor attempted to shove the unreal experience out of his brain, all the while experiencing the surreal feeling of being watched the entire time he continued deeper into the dimly lit hallways. Arming himself with his large, white push broom, the man began sweeping the floor to pick up any larger pieces of dust. While he walked pushing his broom across the shined, cold floor, the realization of dead bodies beneath his feet crept into his mind. His heart rate rose as he continued to feel that somewhat claustrophobic, intense feeling of being watched.

"I felt as if someone was about to pounce on me to attack. I don't know why. I never get that feeling when I'm there alone... I *used* to never feel like that, at least," adds this poor fellow. He watched his reflection become focused in the glass of the entrance door he approached. The blackness of the night made every detail on the man's uniform prominent in the glass. "At the end," he thought to himself as he reached the entrance to the outside of that specific hallway. He tried not to glare at the blackness; it only intensified his phobia-stimulating sense which, at this point, had become unshake-able. Again, a noise broke the silent hallways.

"I heard someone running down the hallway directly across from me. It was running in my direction." He jolted his head up as if he accidentally touched a live wire but saw no one. "The sound of rubber soles stomping at a fast pace advanced in my direction, yet I saw no one." The janitor remained still for a moment as his brain calculated the present experience. "Once the footsteps entered the hallway in which I stood, they stopped." The silence of a large building was again observed. "What is going on here?" he whispered to himself as he placed his broom against the glass door which his back now faced. He kept his eyes moving from side-to-side like a pendulum swing, looking for whomever was in there with him.

"Maybe I should have kept my broom with me," he thought. If anyone broke in, he wanted something with which to protect himself. He was too focused to turn back now. Arriving at the end of the hall, he carefully inspected every area wherein someone could hide. There was no one; he was alone. By this time, the janitor subconsciously returned to the previous topic on his mind: *the bodies*. "Could this place be haunted?" It wasn't too long after he pondered this revelation that he got his answer. While he stood, dumbfounded at the situation in which he found himself, a faint sound cracked through the silence.

"The sounds I heard previously freaked me out a little but, when I heard this, it sent shivers down my spine and arms." The sound of a soft whistle formed around a corner. The tune was unrecognizable. It was slow and lethargic, filled with high notes dropping to low, in-between notes. The sequence of high and low notes created the perfect soundtrack to any "psychopath-killer movie scene." It was out of his view yet perfectly within his ears' range. The stillness of the atmosphere caused his natural breath to amplify in sound. He tried to breathe softer but to no avail. Taking a slow step to the side, the man stuck his back to the wall in hopes of catching a glimpse of whoever was in there with him before they saw him ... if they didn't already see him.

"Who is that? Why are they following me? Is it a kid playing a prank on me?" These questions filled his mind. Our victim managed to trick his mind into believing that it was a "teenage punk." "Darn kid got hold of the ghost stories and knew I'd be here tonight. He probably has a camera and is waiting to jump out at me." He figured it out. Until he quickly turned the corner, facing the whistler to find nothing but a shined floor and walls lined with lockers. Normal school setting, yes, but a teenage punk? No. Perhaps he hadn't solved it yet. Without an answer with which to bribe his uncontrollable nerves, the janitor went back to the safety (so he thought) of the previous hallway and tried to create remedies to soothe his petrified mental state.

The strange noises followed by things being moved and sounds of people walking, as well as vocal cues continued throughout the night. He rushed as quickly as he could, forcing his eyes to look at only that which his cleaning demanded. "The goosebumps stayed with me until I left the premises. I never did see who it was that kept following me. All I know is that something wanted my attention and *it* got it." The janitor found himself moving in a slight jog as he re-equipped the storage closet with the wagon-like can and the rest of the cleaning supplies. He refused to look into the empty abyss of the school as he shut the entrance door and locked it from the outside. "Finally, I'm out, away from that *thing*." He mistakenly thought. He walked to his car, looking forward to getting out of the brisk night wind and enjoying the warmth of his car. Unlocking his car door, he felt the gentle placement of a hand rest upon the middle of his back. He jumped with a gasp as he swung around, prepared to meet the perpetrator. Alas, he was alone, still. "After that night, I vowed to never return to that school at night. To this day, I never have."

A Message from the Forgotten

Since the opening of Erwin High School, it seems that the poltergeists and other forms of haunts wish to weigh in on their "new home." Though the school cannot be entered unless one obtains proper permission, there are areas of the school, such as the football field, which is also reported as a paranormal hotspot, which might be open to visitors under the school's decree. Bodies of the forgotten still rest under the floors of the classrooms and hallways, as they do under the football field. Though their bodies lay lifeless, their souls remain active, beckoning to the living, pleading with us to not forget them.

Witch of the Woods

Creston, Ashe County

The Blue Ridge Mountains: enormous stones, older than mankind itself, powerfully protruding from the Earth's surface, coupled with the spell-like "blue misty haze" which hovers like a permanent cloud over their ridges, creates the illusion of waves frozen in time; delightful to the eye, wouldn't you agree? Some might even describe the pristine view as "spiritual." In the early days of Ashe County's settlement, the solitary valleys and hollows surrounded by the unconquerable mountains served as the breeding grounds for a brand-new culture. A culture wherein European and Native American ways integrate with the spirit of early America. Though hundreds of years have passed since the county's beginning, countless communities exist which still live in this isolated fashion. Endless attributes of the Appalachian culture capture the interest of hundreds of thousands of visitors to the Blue Ridge every year. From the bluegrass or clawhammer banjo picking to the overalls and mountain hats, or even some of the lingo and expressions traditionally used in high country, people from all over the world find a reason to fall in love with the mountains and their folk.

Yet, in the same breath, as one stands overlooking the same scenic wonders, and speaking to the same mountain people, another emotion is awakened. The sense of isolation, completely separated from the rest of civilization, the large rocks and mountain sides bellowing into the sky, and the "ancient" mountain woman or man, silently reclining on a stump or a rickety, hand-made chair looking under her or his eyebrows, watching you as you walk by, instill feelings of unease or anxiety. Why is this? How could it be that a place filled with such awe and peace can harbor the same feelings and

21

A view of Ashe County from Mount Jefferson.

emotions found so often in nightmares (you know, the kind of feelings which turn the simple task of breathing into a labor-intensive chore)?

In the days of old, medicine was a primitive practice (oftentimes, more of a "guess" than a "practice"). That is, when a doctor or practitioner was available. It was the case that many of these rural mountain communities were nowhere near a doctor's reach. When sickness or unexplainable illnesses came upon them, they were left to fend for themselves. The mountaineers were not completely abandoned, however. Specific members of the communities, who were thought to possess a remarkably unique relationship with nature, presented a helping hand. The realization of the relationship these fascinating individuals possessed with nature was first noticed through their uncanny ability to use plants, herbs, and all other things which nature provided as remedies and always knew what object provided what remedy. The uncanny part is, they were usually right. For healing people was not the only reason why people sought these public assistants. It appeared that they contained another unique ability; an ability even more unexplainable; an ability to communicate with the dead. These members of the isolated, mountain communities were always female and each revered lady was dubbed "Granny Witch."

Naturally, merely speaking of granny witches is not enough. I wish to present a more tangible way of knowing the bone-chilling side to these mountain witches, a more *personal* side, if you will. Consider the accounts shared by Mr. Lonnie Benny, an Ashe County native whose grandmother, Madam Bertie Stanley (later married Eastridge) was a highly sought-after granny witch of Ashe County. Shall we continue? If witches don't scare you...

"Her [Madam Bertie] mother died during her early years of childhood and her father worked in coal mines and was never home," states Benny, the granny witch's grandson. "I think that's when her relationship with nature and the spirit world began. She and her siblings were left alone to practically raise themselves."

Madam Eastridge was born in 1917 in an extremely isolated area named Burnt Schoolhouse. Located near Little Horse Creek, the community of Burnt Schoolhouse is in such a rural area of the mountains, it is only accessible by driving on dirt roads which lead up and down steep hollows. Each hairpin turn coupled with the loose gravel pathways force drivers to travel at cautious speeds. The road then abruptly ends. The rest of the journey to the area known as Burnt Schoolhouse must be reached by foot. Needless to say, this section of the mountains defines "rural." It is here where the famed granny witch resided: deep in the wooded, mountainous forest of Ashe County.

"As she grew, people who knew her caught on to her otherworldly abilities. She talked about deceased townspeople as if she knew them, revealing information that only those who knew them in life would know. She was always extremely accurate and never missed a detail."

"How did you know that?" fellow mountain folk (who knew the deceased individuals) would ask her. "*He* or *she* told me," was always the witch's answer. This answer was always met with the same response: silence and the expression of one deeply disturbed.

A Warning from Beyond the Grave

Madam Eastridge's family grew to accept the supernatural abilities of their young member. Her claims were usually met with astonishment and chills as she served as a pathway of communication between the living and the dead. On rare occasions, her claims were met with skepticism. That is, until she undertook a particular conversation with one of her cousins. The queer part about the conversation is that her cousin had died sometime before the conversation took place. The witch was in the midst of conducting her daily work around her family's farm, as was necessary if she wished to survive. In those times, and in those secluded areas, if one wished to eat, one better know how to homestead.

Madam Bertie checked the chickens. "All are accounted for," she thought as she re-latched the coop door, relieved that a bobcat or fox did not visit the chickens for a "late night snack" the night before. Grabbing the sun-bleached handle of the wooden bucket her uncle had made, she made her way slightly down the mountain towards the creek to fetch some water for the squalling egg layers. Nearing the creek, the steady, shallow flow of pure mountain water slightly crashing over the smoothed rocks became louder. She knelt in the cool, thick grass and, placing her hand on the bark of the old oak tree she knelt by, she smacked the creek water with the bucket. Water quickly rushed into the vessel as the current caused it to begin sinking. "Don't fall in!" she thought as she began lifting the bucket from the stream. "I just cleaned thi–."

"Bertie." Her name entered the air from nothingness. "Hello?" Madam Eastridge called as she studied her surroundings looking for her beckoner.

"Bertie, can you hear me?"

"Yes."

Madam Eastridge ceased her pondering as the voice asked this question. It was slightly longer than the first, two-syllable-word which initially caught her attention. She instinctively knew it was the energy of someone whose life had ended; even more, she knew it was her cousin who had recently died.

"Do not let your father enter the mines next week." Madam Eastridge remained silent and attentive. "There will be an accident in the mines. The miners will join *us.*" Bertie Eastridge knew exactly what her cousin meant by "join *us.*"

"How do I force him to stay home?" Madam Eastridge asked the disembodied voice. Alas, there was no response. She waited, standing as still as she could, hoping to receive a response to her burning question. She did not hear her cousin's voice again. The holistic sounds of the water's flow, birds chirping, and occasional light leaf crunch from some small, irrelevant creature served as a reminder of the separation between the spirit world and ours.

Forgetting to reclaim her trusty (maybe even rusty) bucket, the witch ran home and told her siblings everything. Knowing their sister's abilities, they instantly entered a state of panic. Together, they ran to their father, overwhelming him with their unexpected outbursts, "Please! Daddy! Please! Don't go! We need you! Don't go!"

"What is this all about! What's going on? Who's going where?" Their father responded in a high-toned interrogative and exclamatory mixture. After the young Madam Eastridge explained her paranormal encounter to her father, he chose to stay home from the mines. That week, an unexpected collapse occurred in one of the shafts of the mine, the very mine where Madam Bertie's father worked, and killed multiple men.

Turn a Cup

As her childhood vanished into adulthood, her connection with the spiritual world only strengthened. "It arrived to a point where people not only from the community came to meet with her but people from around the county," explains Madam Eastridge's grandson. "When word spread far enough, people came to her asking for guidance and to read their future. Granny witches accomplished this by what's known as 'turning a cup.'"

Bertie Eastridge filled an old copper cup, not much bigger than her hand, with coffee grounds and warm water; just enough to cover the very bottom of the cup. "Ponder that which you came to me to speak about," she would tell her guests as she handed them the cup. Whilst contemplating the desired topic, she also instructed them to gently swirl the copper cup. The witch allowed an allotted time for this process. Slowly and gently reaching towards the individual, Madam Bertie took the cup from the hands of her visitors and with a sudden, single movement, turned the cup upside down onto a tin dish only to lift the cup, revealing the strange patterns and shapes left by the grounds/water mixture. From reading the grounds and shapes created by the substance, she knew what information her guests sought.

A day came wherein a man showed up at the isolated house of the witch. The man, stricken with such fear that he could barely speak, requested the witch "turn a cup" for him. She agreed and sat the man at her usual table used for such occasions. His attitude and state of being was so obviously disturbed that he worried the granny witch. Looking past this, she began her practice as she did so many times before. She filled the cup, gave instructions, waited the proper time, and took the cup back. The man jumped when the witch flipped the cup (not because the impact of the copper meeting the plate on a wooden table was startling but because of the man's uncontrollable nerves). The witch grew curious as to why the man carried himself in such an unusual manner. As she lifted the cup, blood left her face as it quickly turned a deathly pale. After reading the mixture, the witch slowly and consciously lifted her head. "You've killed a man." The witch proclaimed with a shaky voice.

The man clinched his eyes and shamefully hung his head (as if to foreshadow what fate awaited him). "I did. I have just killed a man with a shovel." The man quickly ended his speech. The witch did not know what to say in response to the stranger's confession. The now panicked man erupted from the chair and fled the witch's house unannounced. He was never seen again.

Ghostly Visitors

"Weird things were 'normal things' at my grandmother's home," explains Lonnie. "Things from unexplainable lights to full bodied apparitions were regular occurrences around my grandmother. Often, the apparitions were family members who had died." Lonnie recalls his grandmother, Madam Bertie, telling him that the majority of the hauntings she encountered were not meant to scare her but to ask for help. It appears that most of Madam Eastridge's undead visitors wished to make amends of some kind or another. One such case was that of a man, filled with regret, who turned to Madam Bertie for help. Throughout his marriage, the man conducted himself in truly hateful manners. He abused his wife regularly. As time weathers, so did the man's marriage. His wife had died. After her death, he was filled with shame and sorrow, as if all the weight he acquired through his mistreatments had fallen upon him simultaneously.

The newly gifted pains and agony of this man were yet to be complete. After his wife's death, he began to experience hauntings. The hauntings which left him in a continual state of fear. As these residual curses continued, he realized that his wife had not fully left him. Though dead and her corpse buried, she remained, almost to ensure the man lived the rest of his days in a hellish state. He turned to the witch asking her for guidance but she refused. The man was doomed to reap that which he had sown.

As revealed through her grandson, the witch had a special place in her heart for victims of abuse. As a child, she too was abused, not by her father but by her stepmother, Lot. Madam Eastridge's father remarried after the death of his wife to a woman who, when the children's father traveled for work, would abuse them in wicked ways. This sadly persisted throughout the childhood of the granny witch. Lot's time did arrive, however, and she too expired. During one of the nights shortly following Lot's death, the witch slept, worn and tired from her day of exhausting homestead work. As she lay in her bed, surrounded by nature's chirping and croaking orchestra, she was aroused by the heavy feeling of someone sitting near the foot of her bed. Sporting an expression which showcased her annoyance, Madam Bertie forced her weighted eyes open. Her jaw dropped and her heart began pounding, trading nature's orchestra of bliss for the weakening sound of a fear-filled heart's thuds. Her worst nightmare had returned: Lot was here.

She appeared dead, Lot that is, as she sat near the foot of her bed. Lot's eyes and cheeks were sunken in. Her eyes were so sunken that, due to the darkness of the night, they appeared to be hollow holes in her skull, matching her lifeless face to her loveless heart. The witch lay in a state of trauma as childhood memories escaped her unconscious and became fixed (again) in the forefront of her mind. There Lot sat, in the still, cold, darkness of the night, at the foot of the witch's bed, her lifeless expression staring directly at Madam Bertie; her lifeless corpse remained stiller than still. Madam Eastridge wished it was a dream. Chills formed down her spine as logic screamed, "This is real."

The empty corpse that once was Lot began to operate. There was something unnatural about her movement. She lifted her arm and slowly placed it on her chest, over her heart (if she even had one) all the while, her face, striking terror forever in the eyes of the witch, remained fixed. The holes her eyes had sunken into managed to pierce the witch's soul with horrifying fear's sharpest sword. The body's mouth opened. Without taking a single breath to inflate her lungs, a small voice pierced the stilled moment, "I'm sorry." As soon as the words left Lot's bluish, purple lips, she vanished and the weight which once sat on the witch's bed was lifted, as was the weight that remained in her heart all those years.

The Riddling Witch

Out of the thousands of people who sought Madam Eastridge's assistance, a few of them always stuck out to her. One such memorable encounter was with a gorgeous young lady who came to the witch for guidance. This young lady had planned to elope with her boyfriend. The following Friday, the two planned to meet, alone, on the top of a nearby mountain and leave their community in hopes of starting a new life together. The young lady, whom the witch knew, came to her in hopes of obtaining some level of wisdom regarding her soon to come adventure. What she received instead shocked everyone. In this particular setting, the young girl did not have a private meeting. The witch, along with the young lady, were in the company of others they mutually knew. As various conversations filled the room, the witch began to speak,

> "Riddle to my right.
> On Friday night.
> My heart did ache,
> the tree did shake,
> to see what a hole the fox did make."

Again and again the witch repeated this same riddle until everyone noticed her strange behavior. Eyebrows, slightly slanted, crunched towards the middle of peoples' faces as they pondered the words as well as why she was saying them. Silence filled the room as her words captured the attention of everyone surrounding her. "Do not go to the mountain," the witch told the young girl. "What? Why?" the irritated girl asked. "Do not marry him."

The young woman paused for a moment as she looked at the witch. For a brief minute, she attempted to reason within herself as to why Madam Bertie spoke such a strange and random phrase. More shockingly, why did she advise the woman not to marry her lover? Unable to make sense of it, the young lady left the gathering without thanking her host or bidding a farewell to anyone. Slowly, normal conversations began and quickly filled the awkward air once more as they attempted to forget what had just taken place.

Despite the witch's warning, on Friday morning, the young lady ventured to the top of the mountain where she was to meet her beloved. As she approached the peak, she heard the unmistakable sound of a shovel breaking through virgin ground. Confused, she paused and lowered herself in hopes of not being seen by whoever was digging. She listened for a voice. "Perhaps I'll know who's up there," she thought to herself. She found it rather odd that someone chose to dig a hole there. No one lived around the spot they chose, nor was there a farm around that same peak. After a minute or two of her lowered stance, her legs began to cramp. She slowly raised herself and softly stepped forward towards the sound. One by one, she gently and slowly lowered her weight onto each foot to lessen the sound of breaking twigs and crunching leaves.

As she arrived closer, she saw the back of whoever was digging in such a random spot. It was her fiancé. Her nerves (which were already heightened) slightly relaxed. "What are you doing?" she asked. Her lover did not respond but continued digging. "Perhaps he didn't hear me," she thought. She walked closer to him, this time, normally. Placing her hand on his shoulder she asked, "What are you doing?"

The man paused his digging. It was a large hole, a deep hole. Sweat trickled from the ends of his hair onto his neck. His upper back raised and fell rapidly through his sweat-drenched, white shirt as he panted from his hard work. Using his sleeve, he moved his arm towards his head, perhaps to wipe the sweat from his forehead before facing his lady.

He thrust the dirty shovel into the pile of fresh dirt he made next to the new hole and jerked himself around facing her. "Goodbye," he said as he smiled a sickly sadistic grin. The shine from something clenched within the man's hand caught the woman's eye. She looked down and screamed. In his hand was a knife pointed towards her. The young lady ran towards a nearby tree in a feeble attempt to create a barrier between her and her psychopathic lover. Her mind raced as she thought of what to do next. "If he gets hold of me, there's nothing stopping him from thrusting that blade through me and killing me," she thought to herself. The woman's adrenaline caused her to have tunnel vision. As the man approached the tree, the woman climbed up, not knowing if it would better or worsen the situation.

Climbing as high as possible, she hugged a large branch, hoping that the bark to which her sweaty palms clutched would not give way as she watched smaller pieces descend to the ground. With shallow breaths she began crying and screaming. After a few attempts to retrieve his victim, the man ran in the opposite direction in fear that someone might hear her screams for help. Terrified, she remained in the tree until she was certain the man was no longer a threat. She then jumped from the tree and sprinted towards civilization (e.g., the closest person she could reach) for help. As she ran, she recalled the odd saying of the witch.

Once she reached others, she knew she was safe. She did not

stop running, however, until she reached the witch's house. Without notice, she intruded into Madam Eastridge's home. Crying and hugging the witch, she told the witch everything, "You were right. I should have listened to you. I should've never trusted that fox."

Death Notes

Granny Witch Eastridge occupied a rather normal life. For a witch, that is. "Every once in a while, a bird would fly to her window and peck it with its beak," tells Mr. Denny. "I wonder who it might be this time" was the normal response the granny witch sighed as she watched the bird, or as she knew them "the bearers of news," create its high-toned taps upon her aged window glass and fly away.

"What do you mean?" asked Lonnie, watching his grandmother. An almost visible weight came upon Madam Eastridge each time the bearers of news would visit her. The witch turned to look at her grandson and with a heavy voice, explained, "Each time a bird brings its knocking, a family member dies shortly after." Mr. Denny never forgot these chillingly disturbing words, coupled with the equally chilling expression on his grandmother's face. "Each time she predicted a death in this way, it always came to fruition," explained Lonnie.

Alas, this was not the only way a death note was given to the witch. One night, she was aroused from sleep by the distinct sound of a baby's cry. The cry, which seemed to be coming from inside the granny witch's house, startled her. She quickly rose with attentiveness and began to search each room and corner of her mountain farmhouse (perhaps more comparable to a shack). With ever-growing bewilderment, and the continuing sound of the infant cry, the granny witch walked towards her front door. "Perhaps someone left a child on my porch," Madam Bertie pondered as she gently rotated the front door handle. She slowly creaked the rustic door open as she remained attentive to the cry. The whine continued as she cautiously jutted her head into the darkness of the mountain night. Squinting her eyes, she struggled to adjust her vision to the pitch blackness of the Ashe County wilderness.

Though she continued to hear the crying, she did not see a child before her front door entrance. After closing the door, she scratched her head as, tired, she slowly stumbled back into her bedroom. The infant's crying continued throughout the night. Madam Eastridge was left with only one option: to lie awake and listen to the somewhat disturbing sound of the absent baby crying. The next morning, the witch was given word that a family, who lived in the nearby area, had lost one of their children during the previous night. Yes, Madam Eastridge, through the watchfulness of her bearers of *bad* news, as well as other—more unsettling ways—was able to predict the death of each family member who preceded her. There was one death, however, which she was not given the ability to predict: her own.

In 2015, Madam Bertie Eastridge passed away at the age of 98. The granny witch lived a life of service to others. She created her fair share of medicinal herb elixirs but was more prominently known for her strange epitome with the dead. "There was always a unique feeling at her [Madam Eastridge's] house," said Lonnie. In life, people came, near and far, to visit the granny witch. Though she no longer belongs to the realm of the living, she may very well extend her invitation of assistance. For if you find yourself at the end of an old, dirt road in the depths of Ashe County's mountains, located near an overgrown, forgotten hollow, and dare to wander by foot of the "beaten path" into the ruins of the Burnt Schoolhouse community, you may have a good chance of meeting the soul of Bertie Eastridge, the famed witch of the woods.

Dear Lydia

Jamestown, Guilford County

Each time he crossed under that bridge, a remembrance of that tragic night forces its way into his mind. Though Alexander Thomas desperately fought to keep the sound of screeching tires, the booming crash, and the agonizing screams from replaying, that bridge managed to find the scratch upon the cursed record on which the needle in his mind could not escape. Thomas tried to remember only the pleasant times shared with Lydia. But, he couldn't help but remember her tortuous end. Tears filled his eyes each time the thought of Lydia's untimely end resurfaced from his ever-growing

The bridge where Lydia's ghost is frequently seen.

pile of "forget-m*e-do's.*" Those who knew Alexander reported that the sorrow-filled man often opened disturbing conversations with Lydia whilst alone, almost as if Lydia was somehow still living, "You didn't know what happened at first. I wonder if you even had the chance to ask yourself what had just occurred. How I wish it would have killed you on impact...." After pausing a moment, Alexander offered an apology, stating that his emotions had gotten the best of him. Sadly, time does not permit the turning back of its hands to refurbish the conversational time wasted on his departed Lydia. Oh, dear girl, if Alexander Thomas were permitted such a power as the ability to reverse the hands of time, he would have traveled back to that rainy night in June and saved you—or at least tried to...

Alexander understood that he would never again see Annie Lydia Jackson (Lydia, as neighbors knew her) and always pondered ways to somehow "find peace," as so many people told him he must, without having the chance to offer a proper farewell. He never had the chance to tell her goodbye. He tried not to think about that bit of truth too much. Nevertheless, Alexander struggled for so long, creating ways to finally numb the unimaginable pain in his heart. However, his efforts would come to a head after a very unpredictable event. It was June 20, which is the anniversary of that fatal night, Lydia's fatal night, but nothing more than a particularly lazy day for Alexander. "Xander" (as townsfolk knew him) found himself slopping about his house with nothing but the memory of Lydia's death to keep him company. "I needed to get out. I needed to go somewhere—anywhere," Xander said. He could no longer stand being alone and felt as if he was on the verge of insanity.

Alexander didn't bother making himself presentable. He was alone and too depressed to care what others thought of him. He grabbed the keys to his car and left his cell of isolation to enter another cell of isolation; this new cell was smaller and moved when Xander pressed the accelerator. It was raining. "Funny how time seems to repeat itself," he thought. It was raining the night Lydia left too. He opened his car door and entered. After closing the door, Alexander wiped his wet hands on his already stained, off-white undershirt. After turning on the car, the depressed fellow backed up out of his driveway. After shifting into drive, he paused for a moment to take a breath. "I hoped that somehow that heavy weight I carry in remembrance of you—heavier on June 20th than other days—would magically stay home," he said aloud as if she sat next to him again. Alas, Xander wasn't surprised when he started down the road only to find that his closest friend still refused to leave his side. "I didn't know where I was going, I just needed to go somewhere—go anywhere," he sighed heavily.

The roads were empty; it was a Sunday, Thomas figured everyone must have been with their families, "Must be nice," he thought. "Isn't that a coincidence?" he continued, "Your drive was on a Sunday too." Pretending as if she was there, listening to his words. Alexander drove to a new town—a town he'd never visited. He decided to drive through but not stay long. Alexander didn't like the feeling of not knowing where he was and he didn't feel like asking people for directions. After the main street roads altered back to basic state maintained roads, Xander turned around and headed back. As our fellow ventured back home, that feeling, the deep, unshakable feeling of something missing, grew stronger. It could have been an entity sitting right next to him based on how powerful it became. About midway home, he began to wonder if he ought to take a detour. With it being the anniversary of Lydia's death, the exact day which marked her last, and remarkably similar weather, Alexander thought it might be worth traveling the same road *she* traveled on her last car ride.

"Why not? It wasn't like anyone is expecting me," he thought. Xander took the next left turn to head in the direction of that forsaken bridge. As he drove closer to his destination, the destination which haunted his dreams (through the night or day), he tried his best to replay better memories, happier memories, of Lydia. Alexander hoped that maybe through a strange combination of happy memories and revisiting the bridge, he might finally arrive at that sense of peace everyone told him about. Oh, how wrong he was...

"Should I get out?" he asked himself. It wasn't long before he answered his own question with a resounding "no." It would have been too painful to stand where Lydia's lifeless body lay. As Xander's gaze focused on the bridge, his heart rate increased and he felt a tingling sensation in his fingertips. A similar tingling filled his lips and soared through his cheeks up to his ears. The strange stimuli increased as he grew closer to the scene of Lydia's death. Morbid questions encircled Alexander's head, "I wonder what part of the bridge did her car smash into? How did her driver lose control and how fast was he going?" The morbid thoughts began to turn demented, "Why did fate allow her to suffer moments before she breathed her last?"

As Alexander passed under the bridge, the intensity of the emotions combined with the sadistic questioning caused his vision to become clouded and wavy as he fought to hold back tears, "I don't want to pull over … not here." He said to himself in a wavering voice. Then suddenly his overwhelming state seemed to pause. A momentary wave of relief came over him because of what he saw in the same spot, on which metal and engine met brick. The broken man first noticed the light-brown coloration of her shoulder-length hair. It was curled which made the ends of her hair rest by the bottom of her ears. Next was the white dress.

Alexander could have sworn it was the same white dress *she* so often wore. Except this lady's was not nearly as pristine as Lydia kept hers. Her dress had a large, black streak running across it, as if her dress had managed to get caught on a tire as she rolled it in front of her. To fix a quick flat, perhaps? Smaller, unequal streaks differing in pigment (some lighter, some darker) splattered the rest of her clothing. Though Xander saw her no more than three seconds as he passed under the hellish bridge, her resemblance to Lydia imprinted an image of the woman deep into his long-term memory. For a moment, Alexander Thomas felt happy. For a single moment, he felt like he saw Lydia again.

The brief moment did not last and Xander's extreme state returned to its previous existence of deep sadness, his old friend. He returned home and thought of the woman he saw "Does she know that the very spot she stood in was the scene of someone's death?" he pondered. Again, his mind provided an answer, "No, she couldn't have. At least, she didn't remember it if she did; I'm sure of that." By the time he settled in from his "journey to nothing," it was dusk. Thomas decided to try to get some rest—key word: "try." The next morning arrived, and the emotions and thoughts had lessened back to their normal state of interference. This time, however, a new variable was at play—that girl he saw. Alexander Thomas could not shake the striking resemblance of the woman he saw to Lydia. The more he thought of her the more he remembered, she even appeared to be the same age! Alas, "It is most likely my mind playing tricks on me, replacing features of that lady which I was not able to internalize with your features … what used to be yours." He solidified while returning to his state of lowly existence. Throughout the following week, he could not get the mysterious lady out of his mind. She brought a new sense to Alexander's everyday torment. The more he pondered the strange occurrence, the more fixated he became.

I Can See You

Two weeks had passed since Alexander first experienced the unusual run-in which resembled the dead woman, Lydia. He still struggled to grasp the concept that Lydia was dead. He reminded himself as a feeble attempt to escape his suffering. There are times at random where a strangely familiar thought came to him, "It's been a while since you've heard from Lydia. Why don't you give her a call?" Almost instantaneously, the cold truth of reality again filled his head. Though the chilling truth struck him as a never-ending nightmare, he enjoyed those few moments when he felt as if he and Lydia had simply lost contact, just as old friends do. For some particular reason, he found himself with the ability to breathe easily (though only slightly easier than before). Perhaps, the reason for the ease of Alexander's suffering was due to a conversation he overheard while in town the previous day.

Xander was out running some errands when it struck him that he had nothing prepared for dinner. He scheduled a quick stop to pick up some ingredients before heading home for the day. While he was waiting in line to check out, Xander heard a group of men talking with one of the managers, "Did you guys hear about that girl people have been seeing by the bridge?" His ears became totally attentive when he heard "girl" and "bridge." Thomas continued to listen, "Yes, I did, actually," the manager responded. He continued with a question, "Wasn't that the same bridge that lady died at?" "The same bridge indeed," one of the men answered.

"What do you guys think of it?" By the way the manager was speaking to them, Xander figured they must have been regulars. You know, like that small group of older fellows who sit around each morning at a gas station or general store and converse about whatever comes to mind while drinking and eating crummy coffee and a cheap breakfast sandwich. "I think it's her."

"I do too," agreed one of the regulars. "I haven't seen her myself but, based on what everyone's been saying, it sure does sound like the same girl," responded the manager. As Alexander continued his eavesdropping, he could no longer hold back his curiosity. "What girl and what bridge are you guys referring to?" he asked. They didn't seem to mind.

"There was a bad car wreck a while back over by the bridge near High Point. There were four people in the car. Everyone made it except for one of the girls. That woman died on the scene. I'm not sure what happened to the driver, though. Anyway, it seems that she has returned to the scene of her death. Lots of people who drive under or even by that bridge mention seeing a young lady wearing a white dress with some black oil or tire marks on her clothes. I think they say she has brown hair too."

Alexander felt like his heart stopped beating as an uncontrollable numbness filled every inch of his body. He tried his best to keep his composure. He knew they were talking about Lydia. He knew they were talking about that terrible bridge.

"You all right, son? You look like you're about to fall over!" said the man who was generous enough to fill Alexander in. He tried his best to keep calm. Apparently, he wasn't doing a good job. "Oh, I'm fine, thank you. Just getting over a cold, that's all. Thanks for filling me in. Have a nice day, gentlemen."

"Must have been a nasty cold," one of the men said to another in a hushed tone while Alexander walked away. "Is it true? Is it you? Have you returned?" Questions overloaded the desperate man's man, causing him to feel dizzy. Alexander grabbed as many different newspapers as he could before leaving the market. The second he entered the seclusion of his home, he began, scouring each article, each sentence, each word, until he found them. "DEAD WOMAN RETURNS," "FATAL CAR CRASH VICTIM SEEKS REVENGE," "THE GHOST AT THE BRIDGE," were some of the article titles.

With so many write-ups claiming people had seen Lydia, Alexander began to feel something. A glimpse of that peace, perhaps? "Can you see us, Lydia? Did you choose to stay, dear Lydia?" The now (for the first time in a long time) hopeful man began throwing questions into the empty air around him. From that moment on, he vowed to keep searching for Lydia's ghost until he joined her in her waltz with death.

You Can See Me

A month had passed since Alexander Thomas' ridiculous happenings had begun. His devoted interest in seeing Lydia once more had morphed into a full-blown obsession. He now had an unhealthy, unnatural obsession with connecting with the dead. Over the past month, Alexander occupied his time with attempts to see Lydia, or at least some form of the girl. He listened for her voice and walked around his house, spending time in each room, waiting for her. Despite his efforts, he did not hear nor see Lydia ... yet. "Tonight will change that," the now crazed man said. It took every bit of strength, courage, and whatever else he might have been made of to venture again to that bridge which he hated so much. He knew it wasn't the bridge's fault, but he could not seem to separate it from the woman's dying moments. Alexander planned to bring nothing. No cameras, no news reporters, no extra observers. Just him. He wanted to see her again, alone. He wanted to see Lydia again, desperately.

The Following Morning

Alexander sat, alone, in his darkened cell. This time, he not only observed the silence of the dim room but, also a silence within his mind; he was not tempted to shout disturbing sentences to Lydia. To be quite honest, Alexander wished it were possible to erase all memories of the past month, for his previous state of despair seemed like paradise when compared to this torturous state he experienced. He wanted to vigorously rip all the newspapers containing the ghostly headlines which by now were scattered all over his table, couch, and floor. "I never wish to see them again," he thought, "I never want to so much as entertain the thought of connecting—in any way—with *her.*" He dared not say it aloud but thought about it a lot. Yet, for whatever reason, he softly, painfully spoke, breaking the silence. "Lydia, why? Why has this happened?"

He paused between speaking to think of words that might better express his anguish and annoyance but failed. Perhaps it is because there existed only shadows of that anguish and annoyance Xander once felt. After the night before, a new emotion had replaced the deep mixture of sadness and loss altogether. Alexander Thomas now feared Lydia. He feared her memories which once comforted him. He feared her death. He feared anything that reminded him of the dead woman. Alexander was now filled with a worse haunting. The tormented man looked so desperately for her ghost, for her haunting but received an even more terror-filled realization.

He waited till nightfall. Not because "spooky things come out at night" but because, if Lydia chose to reveal her spirit to him, he wanted to be alone and create yet another, last happy memory. This time, when Alexander arrived at the bridge, he was more resilient than the previous time. He had hoped it was Lydia giving him the extra strength needed to get out of the car. Maybe she wanted to see him too. Xander stopped the car. The slight squeal from the brakes echoed on the arched walls of the underside of the bridge. The only illumination present was that of his headlights and taillights. That is, until he turned the key off. The soothing vibration of the car's engaged engine became silent as he shut the lights off.

When he turned the lights off, the darkness seemed to engulf the car; almost like the darkness was alive.

Alexander paused a moment in the silence, there were no cars around, perhaps for miles. Sitting in his car managed to alter the silence of the night into an even quieter reality. Almost as if he had driven into a painting which depicted an old, beaten-down bridge in the middle of the night, everything seemed to be frozen in time. Alexander cautiously opened the car door and stepped on the cracked asphalt. The smell of wet mud and old tar filled his nostrils as an unexplainable feeling overtook him; it felt almost like broken-hearted nostalgia. Alexander looked around. Nothing filled the empty abyss except for his car and himself. He didn't see *her*.

"How badly do you want to see her?" he reminded himself as he slowly took a few steps separating himself from his car. Alexander's legs began to shake. He was afraid; he could barely see as it was. Though he was looking for Lydia, the fact of the matter was, he was looking for a dead woman. It wasn't long before he saw *something*. The light color helped him see it. Over by the far end corner of the bridge stood something. Alexander squinted his eyelids, leaving a small slit through which to peer. For some reason, he thought it might help his eyes focus. Thomas readjusted his eyesight by forcing them open as wide as he could. The man began his slow pace to the opposite side of the bridge to the corner on which stood *that something*.

"Please don't be a plastic bag," he whispered under his breath as he reached the midway point. Alexander wanted to look back at his car but did not want to risk losing sight of the white coloration. He knew, at this point, if he wanted to return to the safety of his car, he would have to run back to it. The outline of shoulders followed by arms became clear as Alexander silently walked closer. "Could it be her?" he thought to himself. Alexander arrived close enough to see short, semi-curled, light brown hair. The hair was messy, which he found strange. It resembles someone's long hair who hasn't bathed in months. No matter, he knew it was *her*.

"Lydia! It's me!" Alezander exclaimed in a somewhat lowered tone. His heart filled with laughter. He could tell by her honey-brown hair, her favorite white dress, and by the resting position of her shoulders, it was her. It was Lydia. She didn't turn around right away and Xander didn't want to touch her. He didn't know how things work between the world of the living and that of the dead. It didn't take long before he saw her body's weight shift to one side as he heard the soft shuffle of a foot readjusting. Lydia turned around slowly. Xander saw the black marks which now permanently adorned Lydia's white dress. It was her that he saw when he drove past here on her anniversary.

"Oh, Lydia, I didn't see a lady who *looked* like you last time I visited this bridge; it *was* you. There is so much I wish to talk with you about. I've dreamed of th–." Once Alexander's eyes met Lydia's, he could no longer speak, nor could he breathe for that matter. He had never seen eyes filled with such pain and horror. Xander could barely look at them. The unnatural position of Lydia's face as well as the horrible gashes covering her exposed skin caused him to scream. "Who are you? You're not Lydia!" Alexander screamed. Lydia just stood there, looking at him. She looked like a photo; that's how still she was that night. A sobering reminder that she wasn't alive. Nor would she ever be again.

Alexander ran back to his car, dropping his keys around halfway. Once he grabbed them, he managed to run to the car, get in and start it. He looked back and saw Lydia's lifeless expression watching him as he drove away. Still, she didn't move. Alexander Thomas didn't sleep a wink all night. He was left alone, in his cell. This time, he was shaking with fear wondering if Lydia's *lifeless being* would somehow enter his now dark house to haunt him like she did under the bridge. He used to be haunted by her memories, as well as pondering her final moments. Now, he has seen Lydia's final moments and was haunted by that night. If you ever see a woman in a white dress, standing under the bridge near High Point, do not stop. For if you do, you too will share in the horrors experienced by Alexander Thomas.

The Bridge

This bridge still stands. So do the continued reports of Lydia's mangled apparition. Those who see her ghost share the same level of horror and fear as did Alexander Thomas. The haunting of the bridge, which is located in Jamestown, North Carolina, began after the night of Sunday, June 20, 1920, when a Miss Annie Lydia Jackson, who was a passenger along with a C.L. Hutchinson, who ran from the scene, a Nettie Lethco, and a Mr. Cross, crashed a car at the bridge near the town of High Point around ten o'clock that night. Though Hutchinson escaped the crash scene (perhaps the one at fault for Lydia's death?), all passengers and driver survived except for Lydia (Annie Jackson). Over the years, and even today, countless visitors to the bridge report seeing Lydia in her post–car wreck state, as well as capturing unexplainable EVPs and other strange phenomena such as photographs, EMF reads, trigger object interference, and electronic malfunctions. Perhaps our dear Lydia wishes to transfer a message to us, the living, regarding her crash—a message she was never able to present during her final moments.

FAATL AUTO ACCIDENT ON HIGH POINT ROAD

MISS ANNIE JACKSON KILLED LAST NIGHT WHEN MACHINE OVERTURNED.

Miss Annie Jackson, a young lady of this city, met almost instant death last night when an automobile in which she was riding turned turtle on the High Point road at a point about three miles from High Point. The accident occurred at 10 o'clock last night and Miss Jackson died before she could be rushed to a High Point hospital.

The machine was being driven toward High Point and it is reported that the driver lost control on the slippery road while turning a sharp curve. C. L. Hutchinson, reported to be an occupant of the car, could not be found after the accident, and the extent of his injuries were not known, while Miss Nettie Lethco and a Mr. Cross, who were also occupants of the machine, received painful though not serious injuries. Mr. Cross was taken to High Point where a severe cut across his head was dressed, but it was not necessary for him to remain in the hospital. Miss Lethco was able to return to this city last night.

Miss Jackson was about 30 years of age and was employed in a local cigar factory. She is a native of this county, her parents residing in Guilford, and she had been working in the city for only a few months. The body was brought to this city and will be conveyed to the home of her parents for burial.

The newspaper write-up of the car wreck that killed Annie Lydia Jackson, *The Greensboro Patriot* (June 21, 1920).

43

The *Last* Call

Smithfield, Johnston County

Located on East Market Street in the charming town of Smithfield, North Carolina, rests a small yet popular establishment named 'Last Call Bar and Restaurant.' Many recognize this eatery as a trendy place to meet friends over a relaxing beverage and a wonderful meal. Alas, this hangout spot has a different side, serving a different group of people. When owners Kristie (Stehle) and Adam Salem acquired the pub, little did they know that they would share the space with restless souls who had already met their "last calls." Here are Mr. and Mrs. Salem's unsettling encounters.

"We had no idea what we were about to get ourselves into. I've never experienced fear like that until I had the encounter," states Kristie Stehle-Salem, co-owner of "Last Call Bar and Restaurant." She continues, "My husband, Adam, was a skeptic. That is, until he began to encounter the things I did." After reading of their paranormal run-ins, you too will forever remember the unseen presence begging for attention. "Ever since we bought the place, I've always felt as if I was never alone. I can't really explain it. I just knew there was a presence. Sometimes I felt like it was protecting me but other times I felt threatened." According to Kristie, she has always possessed a sensitivity to the supernatural reality.

"We bought a pin-ball machine and that's when things really got out of hand. Every time I walked by it, without missing a beat it would sound off, 'I'm here.' At first, I didn't think anything of it, until I noticed that it only occurred when I walked by." Mrs. Salem goes on to explain that whenever the machine sounded, she was bombarded by an overwhelmingly uneasy feeling, almost to the point of anxiety or claustrophobia. "At this point, I was getting a little freaked out. It was almost like the machine was trying to get my attention." Little did she know, this strange happening was merely the beginning of their troubles.

"Last Call had recently opened. Naturally, we were short-staffed so my husband and I worked almost every shift. We decided to host a karaoke night to bring awareness of our new business. It was a huge success and lasted till about midnight. After we closed, cleaned the place, and prepared everything to open the following day, it was well past one in the morning. So, we decided to crash in the upstairs section (the section wasn't used for anything and there was enough space for a blow-up mattress). After everything was set for the morning shift, we went to bed. Adam woke before I did and went out to get some ice; our ice machine had broken the night before. I woke shortly after he left. It was around 9 a.m. About five minutes after waking, I heard it: 'I'm here.' But, this time, the machine kept saying it, as if it were experiencing some sort of technical glitch 'I'm here, I'm here...' My first thought was that my husband forgot to lock the entrance door and someone found their way in before we opened, which was at 11 a.m."

"I made myself presentable as fast as I could and went downstairs expecting to greet someone. There was no one there. Thinking whoever it was walked towards the back of the building, I checked the bathrooms only to find them empty. By the complete silence in the air, I knew that I was the only one in the room. I then walked to the front door, placed my hands upon the handles, and, with a jerk, checked to see if anyone could have entered. It was locked. As soon as I realized there was no way anyone could have gotten in, it happened again, 'I'm here.' That horrible feeling of being threatened began to kindle within me. I turned to look at the machine."

At this point, Kristie paused for a moment, almost to gather courage to continue the story. One could hear the fear in her voice as she spoke, "When I turned around, that's when I first saw *him*. At the corner of where the bar meets the dining room, was a man dressed in a red coat. He looked to be in the military but not from this era. He had a blank expression on his face; it was almost like he was looking through me. He had light hair and as I looked into his blue eyes, I saw nothing. As my gaze met his, I experienced one of the worst feelings I have ever felt. I was speechless and my heart sank. He just stood there, unnaturally still, almost lifeless. Then, just as quickly as I saw him, he vanished."

"I did not move but listened, hoping to hear someone's footsteps. I thought, maybe he just went to the bathroom. Perhaps my mind was playing tricks on me as a result of exhaustion, at least, that's what I wanted to believe. But it was utterly silent." That is, until something broke that silence, "I'm here."

She scrambled to find the correct key to unlock the front door so she might escape her nightmarish reality. With hands shaking with adrenaline and fingers hanging from clammy palms, Kristie finally located the correct key, enabling her to escape the presence of the breathless apparition. "After I got out, I called my husband and told him what had occurred. He didn't believe me and tried to explain it in every possible way. I know what I saw and I'll never forget it. Once Adam returned, he checked the entire building but, just as I feared, there was no one there." At this point, Kristie knew, without a doubt, that they were not alone. She continued, "It was 10:30 and employees began to arrive. I have never been so happy to have other people in that cursed space. After we opened, I decided to call the man from whom we bought the pinball machine and ask how to turn off the vocal setting."

Her tone of voice changed, "After my conversation with the original owner of the machine, I became truly disturbed." Upon asking the man how to mute the vocal setting, he responded, "Kristie, I don't know how to answer that." "What do you mean?" she asked. "I was confused and a bit annoyed that he didn't know how to operate his own machine." "Kristie," he said, "it doesn't talk." "I quickly ended the conversation. I mean, what else was there to say?"

As she relayed this conversation, the fear and discomfort in her voice was obvious. Since she wished to continue, I listened: "I was thoroughly freaked out and scared. We had a few faithful customers with whom we became acquainted. I decided to tell one of them about this run-in. The man, who happened to be a military veteran, listened. He told me that my description of the apparition I saw sounded like a British soldier from the Revolutionary War." Having researched the history of Smithfield, I was aware of the presence of the British military in the town at the time of the Revolution. I relayed this information to her. Her response was one of shock, almost as if I added to the already established present fear. It is my understanding that the random reminder, "I'm here" persisted after the face-to-face encounter with the King's man. The face-off with the soldier's ghost seemed to usher more activity into the life of the restaurant. As Kristie shared her experiences with others, the encounters became more frequent and stronger. They appeared to be responding to the new attention.

"Most of the time, I felt as if the soldier was only trying to protect me. From what? I don't know. But, as I told others about the phenomenon, I experienced even stranger happenings and felt an unnatural mixture of dread-filled emotions. As I mentioned, I felt protected but there were times I felt so threatened I had to leave." The experiences and emotional torment rose to such a level that Kristie and Adam decided to reach out to the local Roman Catholic Church to ask for an exorcism. One of the priests obliged and carried out their request. It is reported, though strange images and unexplained encounters still occur, they have calmed down and became less threatening after the exorcism.

The Singing Woman

Notice that both Kristie and Adam requested a solution to their otherworldly problems. Do you recall Adam being labeled as a skeptic? Such was true. That is, until he too met one of his lifelong, or should I say, *longer-than-life*, guests.

The Salems often find themselves at "Last Call" in the late hours of the night. Either working on improvements or cleaning-up after events, after hours are the only time in which they can conduct such work. One night, as Adam and Kristie were cleaning after one of their karaoke events, Kristie was talking to Adam about the strange—or even insane—encounters to which she had been subjected. At this point, any talk of ghosts and spooks annoyed Adam, "I didn't really believe in that kind of stuff. It isn't that I didn't believe in an afterlife, it's just, I never bought into the idea that spirits or ghosts could *stick around* like that." Kristie picked up on the fact that Adam would rather talk about almost anything else other than the paranormal at this point. So, the conversation ended and a new one began.

When the couple finished their cleaning and preparations for the next business day, it was the early hours of the morning. They decided to spend the night in the unused room upstairs. As they climbed the steps to the next story, Adam paused to glance at the dining room and bar to ensure everything was in its proper place and all electronics were properly disconnected for the night. After his observation of the room matched his expectations, Adam once again wearily continued upstairs with eyes burning from lack of sleep. The two retired for the night on the air mattress reserved for such nights. The lights were off, all was silent, except for the occasional late-night driver passing through Market Street. Adam took a deep breath and closed his eyes.

"A few minutes passed before I first heard *it*. Having the mind-set I had, I didn't pay attention to it; that is, until it became notice-able." The sound of the radio followed by hushed, murmured conversations emerged from the dining room. "It caught me off guard. I mean, I know for a fact I shut that radio off. It isn't a sim-ple button. It's a switch and I always make sure all sound levels are at zero and the switch is in the off position." Perhaps it was com-ing from outside, he thought. He quickly realized the error in this hypothesis as, at the time, he owned the only business that offered such events. "It had to have been coming from downstairs. I didn't want to wake Kristie. It was a long night and I wanted her to get her rest. So, I just lay there and listened. I wasn't really scared ... yet." Adam couldn't sleep; the sound of people conversing as music played grew louder. "I couldn't really make out what they were say-ing or what music was playing. It [the music] sounded old, but it was all blending together. Kind of like when you enter a room filled with a bunch of people. You hear all the conversations but can't make any of them out."

48

At this point, questions began to flood Mr. Salem's head. He claims to not have been frightened by all the commotion on the first floor until he heard *her voice*. The next unsettling moments of that night would alter Adam's perspective on life after death forever. "I can still hear it, even right now as I'm telling you this. As I laid there listening to everything, a single voice rose from the chaotic sound of multiple people speaking at once and seized my attention. It was the voice of a lady. Her voice sounded heavy, almost sad; she didn't sound like she was crying, just her physical tone of voice sounded sad— perhaps tired, even. That's the best way I can explain it." Through the thickness of multiple conversations and music emerged an eerie, female voice singing. "She was singing the music being played. I still couldn't make out any words. I could just hear that voice matching the rhythm of the mysterious music." The disembodied voice sent chills through Adam.

As soon as he heard the sound of the woman's voice, Adam relayed that only then did he become afraid. "Something about her voice. I can't explain it. The feelings I experienced were like nothing I've ever felt. I was disturbed so deeply to the point of fear; there is simply no other way to explain it." Her voice grew. Not louder, but closer. Adam heard the voice flow through the stairway to right outside their doorway (the door which separated this spare room had been removed, leaving no boundary for safety). "There were no creeks nor steps signifying a body accompanying the voice as it traveled up the stairs. Whoever-she-was stopped advancing once arriving at the doorframe. She stood there, singing." She sang softly and in such a way that Mr. Salem still could not audibly understand a word. Similar to famed musical compositions heard universally, it transcended deep into his mind and heart. Alas, not to instill peace or warmth but heart-wrenching fear!

"My heart rate increased dramatically as she sang outside my room. Vulnerable doesn't begin to explain how I felt. I really didn't know what to do. Each note I heard was slightly off key and lower than it should have been. Then, it stopped." The mysterious woman ceased her singing for about fifteen seconds. "Though it stopped, I was still tense. Then, for a split second, I heard it directly in my ear.

49

As if she was whispering to me." Adam jolted out of bed. Anxiety engulfed his being as he entered a state of panic. "After I checked the room, I laid back down. There was no one in there. I still heard the party going on downstairs but the woman was gone. Let's just say I didn't sleep well that night."

The relief of the morning sun pierced through the window. Adam sat up and waited for Kristie to wake. As soon as she woke up, he told her, "You're not going to believe this but..." "You heard a party downstairs." "You heard it too?" "Yes." "Ok, I believe everything. It's all true."

Kristie did not hear the disturbing voice of the woman. However, she too heard the party or celebration of otherworldly proportions. Perhaps Mr. and Mrs. Salem experienced a time-lapse of sorts in which, for a brief moment, our time and a pastime clashed. Did the Salems experience the unique opportunity to listen in on a party which took place decades ago in the building they now own? Whatever the explanation may be, one thing can be said for certain: "Last

Smithfield's East Market Street. Last Call Bar and Restaurant occupied the storefront on the right of the American Flag. Though Last Call no longer fills the location, the dark energy does.

Call" ensured that *all* of their clientele were welcome. This account was shared with me during the year 2021. Since then, the once popular "get-together" has closed its doors.

Though "Last Call" is no longer in business, Kristie and Adam seemed to have acquired a few hauntings in their personal life. The couple still experience strange and unexplained occurrences. They welcome anyone who wishes to hear the stories firsthand. The sign which once read, "Last Call Bar and Restaurant" stands no more. The building which was once its home remains, however. If you do venture to the present shops which call the buildings on East Market Street "home" and hear the disturbing voice of the Singing Woman, you can say with certainty that you have found the location wherein souls gather to meet their "last calls." Permit me to close this story with a quote from Adam Salem, "I've never heard of a voice of someone who has left this life and entered the next. But, if such voice exists, the singing woman was it."

The Howell Theatre

Smithfield, Johnston County

They say spirits often connect themselves with specific objects or places. Perhaps if a person builds a unique relationship or attraction to a thing or place in life, their soul may linger after death. Others say that ghosts will be present where they have "unfinished business." Whatever the case may be, through the passing of time, the existence of memories connected to places are undeniable. Such is the case for the famed Howell Theatre. Located in downtown Smithfield, this historic movie theater may just have a few guests awaiting a never-arriving final showing. Built in 1935, this theater

The Howell Theatre.

52

has provided entertainment for hundreds of thousands of people. After reading of some encounters by both employees and moviegoers alike, you'll see that some people, or spirits, may wish to watch the rest of the film they never had a chance to finish.

One of the most common "visitors" to the Howell Theatre is the Lost Lady. She is always seen adorned in nothing but a white dress. When she is spotted, she always has her back turned, making her face hidden. Nevertheless, she is frequently observed standing in the aisle or in a row of seats appearing as if she is waiting. She never says a word nor moves an inch and, as quickly as she appears, she vanishes. Consider the following account by one of the former employees of the Howell Theatre:

When questioning the Howell Theatre about the dark and eerie encounters attached to her, one former employee was brave enough to share his chilling experience. Thomas was an employee at the Howell Theatre for roughly two years. He worked there during the summer months as he finished his high school education. Working the closing shifts, Thomas grew accustomed to all the normalities associated with being in an old movie theater during the late night. Might I also add, when the theater closes, only two employees are left to inspect each theater as well as final checks, cleaning, and lock-up. It is usually rather dark because the majority of lights are turned off to signal that the theater is closed.

Thomas was familiar with the closing routines as well as the theater in general but little did he know, he had not yet been introduced to *all* the Theatre's attributes. As Thomas recalls, "The night began like every other night I've ever worked there. I usually worked nights so I got to know the ropes pretty well. After the last customer leaves, I lock the doors and begin the closing shift's duty list. Such was the case with this specific night. After locking the main doors, and making sure the side and back doors were still locked, I began my rounds of checking each theater for anyone who might still be in there as well as any leftover trash. I checked Movie Theater Two, which is located on the bottom level of the building, before starting my way upstairs to check the theaters on the second level. Theater Two was empty and appeared as it did any other night.

"After finishing my rounds upstairs and coming downstairs, I walked past Theater Two once more. This time, out of the corner of my eye, I saw something white. It caught my attention. I stopped and looked. I saw a lady standing in the middle of the row of seats on the left side of the theater. She was looking down ever so slightly. Her presence seemed as if she was waiting for something to happen, almost like something occupied her attention. She was wearing a simple, white dress. I just remember feeling very on-edge and thinking of how quiet that room was though there was a person in it. I don't know; it just seemed too quiet. I also remember how still she was. Not even her dress moved. It was very eerie.

"Despite how I felt, it was my job to make sure she was okay and escort her out of the theater. I'll be honest, I really didn't want to go in there. I could barely see because all the lights were turned off. I slowly—reluctantly—began to walk in her direction. This is where fear's grip began to manifest itself around me. The nearer I drew to her, the fainter she appeared until she vanished altogether. After I couldn't see her anymore, I paused for a moment in an attempt to

Theater Number Two where the female apparition is seen.

54

make sense of it. After about three seconds, I turned around and sprinted out of that theater. I told my co-worker what just happened. It freaked her out too. We finished the closing duties and left the Howell as soon as possible. Usually, after our shifts, we stand and talk outside. That night, we couldn't even think about standing in the vicinity of the theater."

Due to the incredible, spine-shivering encounter, Thomas refused to ever step foot in Theater Two for the remainder of his time at the Howell Theatre. Throughout the coming weeks, validity was added to this claim of Thomas'; as it became clear that heart-stopping encounters, such as the one Thomas experienced, were not happening to only him. Another former employee, Savannah Wilson, was gracious enough to share her story. The encounter Ms. Wilson recalls is one she will never forget. I find it only fit to share a piece of advice, or perhaps a warning: try not to let this story change how you view movie theaters.

Savannah often found herself in situations similar to Thomas. That is, much of her time spent working for the Howell Theatre was comprised of closing shifts. After the two separate encounters they experienced, the two formed a friendship and were grateful they always worked together. They could talk about their traumatizing run-ins. As Ms. Wilson expressed, "I was glad to always work with Thomas. I knew that he wouldn't think I was crazy for telling him what I saw and for being afraid to turn *that* corner." Here is the encounter of Ms. Savannah Wilson:

"The theater was closed. The doors were locked and everyone was out. The other employee and I decided to split the closing list in half so we could get out of there at a reasonable time. It was a new girl working with me so I didn't mind doing things a little different that night. As I mentioned earlier, everyone was out. I was the one to check the theaters. After completing a thorough examination, I was certain no one was left in the building except the other girl and me. Everything was going as expected, that is, until I began sweeping. I started at one end of the lobby, right in front of the restroom, and worked my way towards the center. As I approached the stairway, I saw something out of the corner of my eye. It looked like someone

The original *"Jno. I Barns Funeral Director"* sign located behind what is now the bar of Revival 1869.

Little Girl Blue

"We opened on the 24th of March 2017, and as soon as we opened, that's when the paranormal activity began," state Mike Stojic and Maleah Christie, owners of Revival 1869. Mike continues:

"It was small things at first; we'd enter the front door in the morning to find bottles turned around, loose coins in the cash register neatly stacked, random things in random places. Maleah and I didn't really give these small happenings much thought. I guess that was the wrong response on our part because the strange occurrences became more noticeable—much more noticeable. Since we were still new, we didn't have a large staff. Maleah and I were always there. Once a week, we held staff meetings. One of our former employees had a small child, a little girl, who came with her." Since the meetings were held during the day, before Revival's operating hours, this former employee had no one to watch her daughter. Mike and Maleah were gracious in understanding this and welcomed the small girl to the meetings.

Mike elaborates, "One morning, I arrived at Revival early. I was the only one there. I went to the restroom to wash my hands. The door was shut behind me and, as I was washing my hands, I heard the sound of a little girl softly speaking a few words then giggling. My immediate reaction was a greeting. I yelled out, 'Hi, I'll be right out.' I didn't hear a response. I opened the door and saw that the room I faced was completely empty."

"A bit confused, I walked around calling for the employee and her child. Again, I never heard a response. I checked the doors; they were still locked. I sent a text message to this employee to ask if she had arrived. Within a few minutes, I received a text from her which read, 'Sorry, I'm stuck at a red light. I'll be there in five minutes.'" Mike's hands felt clammy as his confusion turned to shock. He continues, "I know I heard a little girl. I mean, she was directly on the other side of the door. Almost as if she knew I was in there and wanted to get my attention. I tried my best to not let this experience bother me and managed to keep my composure during the meeting, but, I admit, it really freaked me out."

Mike told Maleah, his business partner, about the confusing experience he encountered. Maleah, too, found it rather strange. The

Revival 1869's patio.

two didn't give it much thought. The idea of a supernatural explanation never crossed their minds ... until a couple of weeks later. What they found one morning, covering their patio, is enough to deeply disturb anyone.

"Two weeks went by after I heard the little girl's voice. We were especially excited for tonight's shift because we had the patio pressure washed the day before. It was a beautiful, spotless white. Maleah didn't get a chance to see the finished work. Since we were at Revival prior to opening, we both eagerly walked towards the patio entrance to view the ultraclean finish. We opened the door and what we saw covering the patio managed to scare both of us. Covering the patio were five-inch-long, bare footprints. These prints were not like normal footprints. There was no direction or pattern and, in some prints, the toes on the left and right foot were opposite one another. As in, the feet were facing opposite directions. To make matters worse, we found prints in places on the patio that would be absolutely impossible for someone to stand on—even a small child. We found prints on the physical entrance to the patio. In order for someone to stand there, they would've had to unlock the door, open it, and stand in the doorway."

Mike and Maleah were shaken to the core at the sight of these unexplained footprints. The prints were unlike anything they had ever seen. The night before, Mike and Maleah, along with other team members, left the premises around 1 a.m. To add more confusion, the owners are very stern in their rule "strictly 21 and older may enter Revival 1869." After a careful observation, they quickly realized that there was no true explanation for this phenomenon. After reviewing the surveillance footage of that night, no one was seen on the patio. The cold footprints remained as patio decor for months to come.

"At this point, we began to wonder if something more was going on here. Between the oddly placed bottles, loose change stacked, the girl's voice, and now the footprints, we began to wonder if maybe we weren't alone." This new revelation came exactly at the right time, as someone was about to see this mysterious entity face-to-face.

"It was a really good night. We had a full house and everyone appeared to be enjoying themselves," states Maleah, "Everyone seemed to be having a good time until I was approached by a group of customers with a complaint that I'll never forget." Walking through the crowded room were four adults. This group of four were two couples who met over some drinks in the lounge. They also happened to be loyal regulars. I happily greeted them but they seemed a bit bothered. I asked, "Is anything the matter?"

"Well, yes, actually. I love that you guys have a 21-and-up rule here. In fact, that's one of the reasons why we come; it gives us a place to relax and know that children will not be running around. I just wanted to inform you that there is a little girl roaming around from room to room."

Maleah felt agitated that a customer refused to respect their rule. "Thank you for letting me know. Can you point her parents out to me?" "Well, that's the thing, she isn't with anyone. She's just walking around by herself. She has blond hair and is wearing a blue, smock-style dress. She looks to be around five years old."

At this, Maleah became all the more upset to hear that not only did a customer disrespect Revival's rule, but also allowed a child to walk around unchaperoned. Maleah describes the following account, "After ending the conversation with the two couples, I immediately found Mike and told him what was happening. He was offended by this as well. We both began searching for the little girl—and when I say 'search' I mean we looked everywhere. But we never found her."

Later that night when the formerly crowded room was filled only by the employees cleaning and preparing the establishment for the following day, Mike and Maleah checked the surveillance cameras. A little girl never entered Revival ... nor did a little girl ever leave. After reviewing the footage and learning this, the partners froze in their seats as they felt a wave of fear once they finally understood what was happening. That night, they finally accepted the reality that is the ghost of Little Girl Blue.

Friend or Foe?

How would you react once discovering that the building in which your livelihood resides is haunted? It is the normal response to feel on edge. You might feel as if someone is watching you so closely that, at any moment, you'll feel a cold, lifeless hand reach from behind you only to rest upon your shoulder. Maybe fear overtakes you at the news of sharing space with a lost soul. Once you read of the next restless soul haunting Revival 1869, you might have considered the presence of Little Girl Blue to be the least of your troubles.

It was soon after Revival's grand opening. The shift went as expected and the bar closed at 12 o'clock midnight. The energy-drained team cleaned, prepared for the following work day, and locked the doors. "We decided to go out on the patio to chat and unwind," Maleah states as she prepares to share one of the most frightening experiences of her life.

"Once closed, the team, Mike, and I occasionally sat outside to talk and relax a little before going home. It gave everyone a chance to get to know each other better and let go of any stress collected throughout the night. As we conversed, I checked the time and saw that it was now one in the morning. A whole hour managed to race by without any of us realizing. Since we were still a new business, Mike and I wanted to set good standards. So, I ended the conversation. 'Everybody out,' I said as I directed everyone back through the door from the patio and to the main entrance and exit of the building. Once we found ourselves standing outside of the main doors, I went back in, alone, to take a quick walk-through and make sure everything was set. As expected, everything was in its proper place and the only lights remaining on were the floor lights used to softly illuminate the walkways when the room is dark.

"As I began to exit, I noticed one of the men standing at the end of the bar. He had a beard. So, I figured it was either Mike or one of the other employees at the time. 'What are you doing in here? I told everyone to head out.'" He didn't respond. He just stood there, looking at me. Since the floor lights were still on, I could see that he was wearing a white, buttoned-up shirt, a barber's shirt. He was pale, but the part that really freaked me out was the expression on his face—or lack thereof. Since he didn't respond, I noticed myself getting angry as I walked back outside to conduct a head count and find out which one decided to "be funny" at 1 a.m. "After I finished the head count,

I couldn't speak. Everyone, including Mike, was still outside, waiting for me."

Mike chimed in to share his perspective. He recalls, "Her complexion seemed as if all of the blood had left her body. I've never seen Maleah that scared before."

"I looked back inside towards the direction in which the man was standing. He was gone and, since all the doors were locked and only I had the key, the remaining way out was through the doorway in which I was standing. I saw a man that night who wasn't really there. At least, not like you or me," said Maleah. This experience would go on to haunt her for weeks to come. Unlike Little Girl Blue, both Maleah and Mike report that there is a kind of agitated aura that accompanies this apparition. After Maleah's frightening encounter, a paranormal phenomenon was at the forefront of potential answers for what was happening at Revival. As you continue to read, you will find that they were exactly right. The following accounts suggest the lifeless man Maleah saw that night wanted to inform the two that he *had a say* in what happened to the old building...

"I got into the habit of pouring a glass of whiskey and playing the piano at the end of the night, when everyone is gone. It allows me to decompress before heading home myself. Maleah had already left, all the doors were locked, and I was completely alone in the middle of the night with a glass of liquor and a piano. It was going to be relaxing ... or so I thought. Shortly after I began to play, I saw a man walk past the doorway. I was able to catch a glimpse of him. He wore a white shirt and sported a beard. As soon as he passed by, an instinct kicked in." Mike went on to explain this instinctive feeling, "I served nearly nine years in the United States Marines. My first deployment was to Iraq from 2006 to 2007. My second deployment was to Afghanistan in 2013. Needless to say, I've learned how to read dangerous situations very quickly. When you are in those kinds of situations and something bad is about to happen, you get this *feeling* that puts you into 'fight or flight.'

"It is difficult to explain but, that instinct is what I felt immediately after I saw this guy. I knew he wasn't a friend. I didn't see nor hear anything after he walked past the doorway. So, my military training kicked in. I began to clear each room until I found him. My first thought was that someone broke into the bar. I finished clearing the entire building. There was no one in there. I still had that 'you're in trouble' feeling and couldn't understand why. I quickly turned off the lights, locked up, and left. As soon as I left, that feeling went away. I don't spook easily but that night genuinely scared me."

The male ghost that both Maleah and Mike have now encountered sent a very strong message: he did not like them there. After sending his message, the troubled soul sent another sign but, this time, it was physical. How quickly a good time can turn frightful in the blink of an eye!

A group of ladies sat at the bar. They delighted in a conversation with the owners as they enjoyed their mixed drinks. All was normal until a loud crash and four, female screams were heard throughout Revival. As the conversation between owners and patrons continued, a pack of soda cans, which were stored near the section of the bar where the ladies sat, began to violently fly through the air in the direction of the customers. "The cans leaped into the air in the same way as if someone lost their temper and, with their arm, cleared a table, sending the contents across the room." Maleah and Mike explain as they consider the situation. The ladies jumped from their seats and ran to the other side of the room, screaming.

This attack was witnessed by everyone in the room that night. It left the expanse utterly silent for a moment as people wrestled to find some explanation as to what had just taken place. Everyone was left without a thought, completely dumbfounded. That is, everyone except Mike and Maleah. The team knew exactly what had just taken place and who was responsible. Only one question remained, "What do we do from here?"

As time continued, news of the strange phenomena occurring within the walls of Revival became far reaching. Among the numbers was a psychic and a paranormal investigator. Both men approached Maleah and Mike with a single question: "Do we have permission to investigate?" Desperately searching for answers, Mike and Maleah gave permission in hopes that the psychic and ghost hunter might be able to relieve the team with answers. "We kept our mouths shut and were sure not to give them a single hint. At this point, all they knew was the basic stuff," states Mike as he retells the interaction.

"Maleah and I agreed to not tell them anything. If they were fake, we wanted to be the ones to expose them. We settled on them coming in after hours. The two men inspected each room. Once they were finished with their investigation, they revealed what they discovered." After hearing the following description of what the psychic read during his time there, Maleah and Mike were paralyzed with terror as they finally came face-to-face with their worst nightmares.

"There are two prominent spirits here," the psychic told the owners, "One is a child. I feel that the child is a little girl. She's harmless, wants to get attention from those willing to give it. I wouldn't worry about her. But, the second one... I can tell I am being watched by a hostile, male presence. He doesn't want me here."

"That is exactly the same conclusion to which we've arrived." replies Mike and Maleah. After the investigation, more news of the haunted bar and lounge became widespread. As interest grew

A view of the Ava Room in Revival 1869.

among the customers, employees, and owners, Mike and Maleah decided to start connecting with the spirits in hopes that they might be able to give them their sought-after attention. Although the negative energy can still be felt, the burning anger that was once observed has lessened.

The supernatural activities which occur at Revival are countless. There are simply too many to mention in this book. Mike and Maleah preserve footage and photos of the terrifying events for their guests. They welcome anyone to ask about these encounters and the evidence they have collected over the years. People leave the location with mixed opinions. Nevertheless, one thing is certain: Revival 1869 stands as one of the most haunted locations around Clayton, North Carolina.

The male poltergeist is believed to be Mr. Ross Duncan. Before the fabrication of the brick building, Mr. Duncan owned and operated a wood, Victorian barber's shop which unfortunately burned down. Mr. Duncan's shop stood at the exact site where Revival's bar counter now rests. As for Little Girl Blue, just be sure to agree if she asks to play with you.

The Show Must Go On

Benson, Johnston County

Imagine, if you will, an old theater filled with the most dedicated of performers who willingly exhaust themselves in musical performances and dramatic shows. The audience adores each performer and the theater itself, yet there is a strange hesitance in the air, a mix of fear and precaution shared by both audience members and performers. The reason for such a strange blend of emotions is due to the phantom which haunts the beloved theater. All the actors and actresses know of the stories; some have even seen him. The same can be said for the dedicated lovers of theater among the nightly audiences. Does this story sound familiar? Don't be surprised if it does. Countless tales exist such as the present one. These tales grip millions with fear but, for some unexplained reason, capture their hearts as well. I wonder, would the same outcome of fear and love be observed if the tales were true? What if there really was a phantom (or phantoms) who haunts the theater? What if I told you that the exemplified tale I shared with you earlier was not a tale but based on an actual theater? Perhaps the heart-capturing effect invoked by the tale would turn heart-stopping. May I introduce you to just that, a truly haunted theater?

Located on East Church Street in beautiful downtown Benson is the W.J. Barefoot Auditorium. The theater holds countless memories. However, not all memories coincide with the common happenings related to "theater life." The auditorium is also a place where older generations reminisce of their school days. Once called Benson High School, the building which is now the W.J. Barefoot Auditorium was built in 1918. The school closed its educational doors and opened its doors for entertainment in the year 2000. Although this building

The entrance to the W.J. Barefoot Auditorium.

holds fond memories, there exists an undeniable force that causes certain individuals to refuse to enter the structure alone. There are people who strongly reject the notion of even sitting in the auditorium by themselves, and quickly change topics if questioned about their caution. Strange occurrences happen in all manners; some small, only revealing the dark side of the theater to a chosen person; others larger, reminding an entire cast that they are not alone ... like the encounter I am eager to now share with you. I invite you to partake in the experience which left one cast with permanent stage fright!

"It was 2015. I was just a teenager at the time. But this is something that, even to this day, seven years later, still gives me chills," states Jimmy, a lead in the present musical. "My girlfriend at the time, along with a handful of other performers, were in almost every show they [the theater] put on." So, we knew the theater better than anyone else. That means, we knew the stories about "the people upstairs." You see, the theater was once the original Benson High School. It was renovated but only in certain parts. There were

One of the "frozen-in-time" classrooms at the W.J. Barefoot Auditorium.

untouched places in the building that still had classrooms, school materials, even names on the walls from the 1950s. It was kept off limits to most people. But, since we spent so much time at the theater, we knew how to get to the upstairs sections. One night, after rehearsals, my girlfriend, a few friends, and I decided to venture into the dark, time-capsule–like rooms. Rehearsals for the show got over late, around 10:30–11:00 at night. As soon as we entered the untouched area, we instantly felt a sense of foreboding. Being teenagers, we chose to ignore it. I wish we hadn't... We walked around the rooms and took note of everything we saw: tables, pencils, chalkboards with original chalk; some boards even had assignments and teachers' notes on them. The thing that caught my eye was the names and dates written on the walls. There were so many and they ranged from the 1920s to the 1950s. Some in ink, others in pencil.

After looking around for some time, we got comfortable in the almost completely dark space. Foolishly, we decided to try and get a reaction from the ghosts that supposedly haunt the theater. I decided to knock on the wall in a pattern which all generations know.

I knocked five times and waited for the response, which would have been two knocks. The five knocks echoed through the eerie hallways and vanished into silence. I did this two more times. Then, I decided to sing the "jingle" which traditionally accompanied the knocks. As I knocked, I called, "Shave and a haircut..." and awaited the two-knock response. We stood in the silence until we heard it, "Knock ... knock." Immediately, the joking and teenage laughter was exchanged for adrenaline and anxiety. We stood there, whispering as quietly as we could, "Did you hear that too?" "Did that really happen?" Then, we heard it again, this time, it was coming from another area.

"The space was so quiet that I could hear my own heartbeat. We felt as if whoever was knocking wanted us to follow. Every time we heard the knocks, it was in a slightly different section, until we came to a room we hadn't previously explored. As we approached the room, the knocking ceased. There was something about that room. We all began to feel as if we were in danger. It was a strange feeling. 'BANG!' We heard an unmistakable, loud slam as if someone had just reared his or her arm, fully extending it behind, and flung it

The forbidden section within the W.J. Barefoot Auditorium.

forward, slapping the wall as hard as he or she could. We dashed as quickly as we could out of the foreboding area. When we came out from the closed-off sections, we looked around thinking that someone was messing with us. Much to our fear, we remained the only *living* people in that area of the theater."

Jimmy, his girlfriend, and their friends never went to that section in the same fashion again. They clearly understood the message so strongly given: "You have no business here." From that moment on, it was not uncommon for individuals to bring a second person to the costume storage which is directly across the hall from this apparently guarded area. Alas, this was not the only time that the group had an otherworldly interaction.

"We were rehearsing for a show," explains Jimmy. "It was 'tech-week' which is the week before the actual performance. This is the point in which everyone's nerves begin to surface. No matter how many shows any of us had been in, there is no form of preparation that would prepare someone for what we heard during that week. The show in question was set in the 1950s. The clothes, dances, and music resembled that which was common at the time. I guess that fact must have triggered *something*... The scene we were working on was the section in which I made my entrance. I was the lead, playing a famous rock star. When I arrived on stage, everyone began singing this anthem which, as the script read, was shared among the members of the fan club. As I stood in the middle of the stage, everyone began singing. However, something was off and everyone heard it."

"There was a voice, slightly delayed and not quite on key, which was singing with everyone. Since all of us heard the voice, it could only mean that the person to whom the voice belonged had a microphone. Mind you, this is during tech-week, all jokes and games must be put aside during these important, last rehearsals. The voice was strange, even spooky. After we finished singing the anthem, the director stopped the rehearsal to find out who was so off. After checking the microphones and undergoing a vocal check, we determined that the voice came from someone backstage. The creepy part is, no one backstage had a microphone. The director marched backstage to find out who was singing. No one in the back heard anyone singing in such a macabre fashion. The thought that a person, no longer living, was singing a song that was directed towards me bothered me for a few days. Quite honestly, it still bothers me, these eight years later."

Hearing a disembodied voice singing to you is enough to cause anyone to feel a deep sense of dread. Encountering a spirit that wishes to be left alone is an experience that people who have faced it wish to never face again ... if they're lucky. The fact of the matter is Jimmy's encounters were not the only time a ghost gave a powerful warning. Here is an encounter with another ghost, or perhaps the same ghost, who does not want to share the spotlight. After reading Mrs. Hernandez's encounter, you can decide for yourself if this ghost is performing a solo or if the haunt carries an ensemble.

B.J. Hernandez served on the planning board at the W.J. Barefoot Auditorium for a period of time. Her encounter occurred as she was actively serving. The story about to be shared with you is one of the most anxiety-provoking, paranormal encounters anyone could experience.

"It was January of 2019," states Mrs. Hernandez. "I was alone in the theater's lobby talking to my mother on the phone. The doors were all shut and locked. My mother and I were having a serious discussion concerning a family matter. Coincidentally, emotions were high. I was completely engulfed in the conversation until something snapped me back into my surroundings. A large, metal door slammed shut behind me. I felt as if I was going to jump out of my skin! As soon as it slammed, I felt an unusual feeling. I felt as if I was being followed. The feeling started very small, almost like a sense. It quickly grew to an overwhelmingly anxious suspicion as if someone was aggressively chasing after me and was so close that, at any moment, they were going to wrap their arms around me only to throw me to the floor. The emotions I felt while speaking with my mother were quickly replaced with panic and fear. I abruptly ended the discussion with my mother and began to exit from the lobby. All I could tell was whoever was in there with me wanted me to leave."

B.J. continues with hesitancy: "I don't know who is there but I'm leaving now!" I desperately opened the doors to exit the lobby. As I opened them to leave, another door slammed shut. To this day, I won't go into the lobby alone. Neither will I ever forget the ghost who so strongly despised my presence. "I don't know who it was but one thing is for certain: that was one of the scariest things to ever happen to me!"

Mrs. Hernandez ran to the auditorium for safety from the *thing* which pursued her. Little did she know, the auditorium is also a place where spirits know no boundaries. The auditorium itself serves as a paranormal hot-spot for the location. There have been so many active sightings that some people, who have shared countless hours on the stage, refuse to sit in the auditorium for fear that they might fall prey to the lurking shadows. I invite you to consider the frightful account of Shayna Tucker, a seasoned performer and staff of the W.J. Barefoot Auditorium.

"It was May 8th, 2022. The show had just ended. The cast was tasked with striking the set which means to break the set down and ensure props are in their proper places. It was a large-scale show, so it took us a while to finish. It was about 10 p.m. by the time we completed the strenuous task. As the cast shared their final good-byes, we all left the theater. A few members of the cast and I decided to go out for a late dinner. As we neared the end of our meal, we found ourselves in deep conversation. Not wanting to end our memorable moments just yet, we decided to return to the theater and reminisce about the months-long work on the show which was officially over."

"We returned to the now-empty theater parking lot and made our way back inside. We sat in the front row of the auditorium. The morale was high as we shared meaningful stories and fond memories of rehearsals. That is, until it was all interrupted.... SLAM! Our hearts paused for a short time as we registered the sound of the backstage door violently shutting. Frozen in fear, we stared at each other's pale faces. After all, we were the only ones in the building. We dashed to the emergency exit to escape whoever—or *whatever*— was so angry. We managed to escape and found ourselves outside. As I held the door open, we yelled into the theater, 'Hello? Who's backstage?'" "There was no response. I slammed the door closed. We made our way to the backstage door in an effort to investigate the possibility of another person entering. It was locked and the parking lot was still empty. Though this wasn't my first meeting with the ghosts of the theater, it was the first time I felt in danger from them. I didn't return to the theater for months."

This was not the first meeting Ms. Tucker experienced. The first time she had the unwanted pleasure of meeting the phantom— or phantoms—had a much greater effect on her; one that would shape a new perspective of "theater work" and ultimately, mortify her:

"During the summer of 2019, I was on staff at the theater, working with a musical summer camp. During this time, there was one night in which we, the staff, stayed late to get things ready for the following day. It was about 11 p.m. We were all working on our assigned tasks when something red in the curtains of the right-stage-wing caught our attention. A little girl wearing a red dress mischievously stood by the curtains. Surprisingly, none of us were shocked. We (the staff) gave this little girl the name 'Shelly.'" When Shelly is seen, it only means that more activity—stronger activity—is to follow. We quickly stopped our assignments and packed up our belongings in a last-minute attempt to outwit whatever lifeless fate awaited us.

"The soundman needed to shut off the power in the sound booth before leaving. Having just seen Shelly, he didn't want to go alone (the sound booth is located upstairs, in the back of the balcony). A few brave volunteers and I agreed to accompany him to the sound booth. Looking back, I really wish I hadn't agreed to go... We turned the corner, facing the darkened, old stairway. We looked towards the top of the stairs only to find a tall man standing at the last step. He looked like he knew we were coming and was waiting for us. He began to advance deeper into the balcony, almost like he was ushering the way for us. I felt like my heart stopped. We wanted to turn back and leave but all of us would have received penalties for leaving the sound booth activated. With great reluctance, we huddled together as we made our way up the stairs.

"We approached the top of the stairs only to find that the man was not there. We glanced in the direction of the stage. Shelly was still in the curtains. Shaking with fear and adrenaline, we made our way to the sound booth. My legs felt numb. We turned the second corner to the sound booth. Inside was the man. I was too scared to scream. The soundman flung his arms into the booth and switched the power button to 'off.' Without missing a beat, we flew back down stairs, finished gathering our belongings, and left the theater. I love musicals but I was never happier to leave than that night. As we drove away, I glanced back to look at the theater. Shelly, the man, and another girl were standing, stiller than still, watching us leave through a window located on the second story in the forbidden, untouched section. I'll never be able to get that image out of my mind."

Those who work at the theater have given the name "Bob" to the tall, male apparition. To this day, Bob and Shelly are periodically spotted. It is not uncommon for the staff to credit these two ghosts with the unusual noises or falling objects which spook audience members from time to time. Staff members who have had the opportunity to meet the *chilling* individuals report that it seems

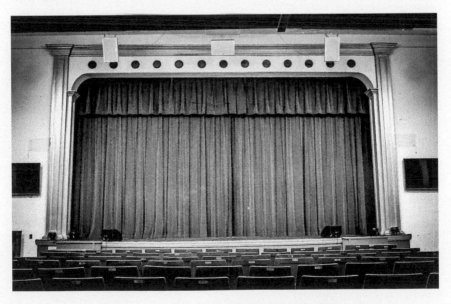

The stage in the W.J. Barefoot Auditorium.

the ghosts are most active when they are tired of visitors and feel as if one's time in *their* domain should be over. It is thought that Bob is one of the original teachers of the old Benson school and refuses to leave his post. Shelly is thought to be a young performer who refuses to make her final curtain call. Naturally, these are speculations. Only one thing is for certain: if you find yourself in the W.J. Barefoot Auditorium, be sure that you are well behaved and follow the school rules. If you choose not to, Mr. Bob may just have to remind you...

The Silenced Boy

Clayton, Johnston County

The year was 2016; 135 years after the first lifeless corpse was entombed in the Clayton City Cemetery. The resting grounds are quiet and peaceful—or so Cassi thought. The young mother and her son, two years old, used to walk through the hallowed space on their daily commute into town. It was a restful period of their walk since cars rarely entered the decrepit graveyard. Usually, Cassi allowed her son to explore for some time before continuing their daily travel. This would all change on the day—the *last* day—Cassi and her son, Gage, ever set foot in the cemetery.

Cassi and Gage began their daily routine just like every other day. They woke up, ate breakfast, fed the dogs, horses, and pigs, and readied themselves for their normal, 30-minute walk into town. Cassi breathed a relaxing sigh as she and her son reached the moss-covered gates which served as means of entrance to the cemetery. Pushing the gates open, they happily entered the resting grounds. The mother gazed at the headstones, tall grass, and weathered trees as the boy curiously picked the grass at her feet. There is a particularly large marker which always caught Cassi's attention. After enough strength was gathered to complete the remaining portion of their journey, Cassi and Gage left the calming space and advanced towards town.

While in town, the mother and son ran into old friends with whom they delighted in a lengthy conversation. Due to the length of the discussion, Cassi and Gage were behind in their normal schedule. It was dusk by the time they found themselves facing the gothic-like gates again. Day or night, the cemetery was a special place for the two and invoked feelings of peace when resting within her walls. Innocently, they entered the gates. All was normal until Gage

The plaque marking the entrance to Clayton City Cemetery. Notice the orb-like phenomenon captured within this photograph (located on the upper section, center right, of the photo).

The gates of Clayton City Cemetery.

pointed and began to speak. "Mom, who's that?" Looking towards the direction in question, Cassi answered muddledly, "Who's who, Sweetie?" "The boy right there." Noticing nothing but the empty space before them, Cassi paused in confusion then answered, "What are you talking about? There's no one over there." Gage eagerly replied, "Yes, there is! That little boy in all white. He's telling us to go over there." At this remark, Cassi's heart began to speed as her motherly instincts took over. "Gage, there is no one over there."

"Mommy, he's looking at us and wants us to go over there. He looks sad." "Gage, you're scaring mommy, cut it out." Gage didn't say anything. Noticing the silence, Cassi broke her attention from the empty space to glance at her son only to find an expression of bewilderment and concern covering the boy's face. "What's wrong, honey?"

"He's trying to talk but he can't; his lips are sewn shut." At this, Cassi began to panic. Her mind fogged, she was unable to respond. Against her will, but trying to do what's best for her son, Cassi walked Gage over to the corner in which the *other boy* was beckoning to prove that there was no boy standing there. As they approached the corner, Gage did not claim to see him. But, what Cassi saw would

The Clayton City Cemetery.

The aged and weathered graves at Clayton City Cemetery.

be enough to erase any positive emotions attributed to the cemetery. As she looked down, she saw a headstone; on it was the name of a boy. The dates forever etched into the marker indicate that the boy was the age of her own son.

Cassi, already clutching Gage's hand, abruptly left the cemetery and, holding her son, ran home. After they arrived home, she handed the child to his father and stepped outside hoping to somehow make sense of the utterly terrifying conversation with her son. She was never able to let go of what her son told her that night and taking time to think about it only made the realization that her son saw a ghost more believable, "How could Gage know that they sewed the mouths of the dead shut? Why would he say the boy was wearing white?" Cassi and Gage never set foot in the Clayton City Cemetery again. Though years have passed, Cassi remembers that numbing night clearly and avoids the forgotten grounds entirely. Cassi and Gage learned quite the lesson that impossible night: Be careful when you open the old gates of a cemetery. Because, there might be something—or *someone*—waiting for you...

The Poltergeists
at Riverside

Smithfield, Johnston County

By the time we left the Riverside cemetery, my blood was chilled as cold as that frigid night's air. This experience happened when I was about 15 years old. I *used* to ghost hunt back then. But, it's run-ins just like the one I am preparing to tell you now that brought my "paranormal investigation days" to a halt. Heed my warning, if you scare easily, this story is not meant for you. As I record this account, I find myself pausing frequently to glance behind me, thinking they've found me; no one's there. It's just that suffocating feeling returning as I relive in my mind that terrible experience...

The cemetery is in a beautiful location just alongside the Neuse River. I guess that's why it's named "The Riverside Cemetery." Established in 1777, this graveyard is the resting place of countless people. After we were forced to end our investigation, we learned that the souls fixed to the mysterious grounds will ensure that they will never be forgotten. We waited till the sun had completely fallen and the darkness of night fully took over. My paranormal team, six of us including myself, prepared our equipment to begin our efforts of connecting with the dead. We approached "Riverside" cautiously on that late October night, as we scoped out the area. We entered the cemetery.

"Hello?" Immediately, we froze in place and snapped our heads, pointing our eyes in the direction of the disembodied voice. It was a little girl's voice. "Did you guys hear that?" I said as I looked back at my team. "A little girl just said, 'hello,'" they responded. The voice came from the location of a bush. There were no animals nor living

Riverside Cemetery, established 1777.

people, other than us, in the cemetery. After a short discussion about the ghoulish welcoming, we continued forward, deeper into the cemetery, accompanied by nothing but the blackness of the night. We found ourselves by a small, white mausoleum. We decided to rest for a moment.

We conducted a few EVP sessions and wanted to see if any recordings revealed a voice from beyond the grave. Alas, something didn't like the idea of us resting against the mausoleum. My back was pressed against the ice-cold brick as I gently laid my head against the grave, "Tap, scratch, tap, scratch, tap, scratch." Right next to my ear was the sound of a weak finger, struggling to tap from the inside of the mausoleum. I jerked my head and body off the grave as I desperately tried to stop my mind from replaying that horrifying sound. My sporadic movement startled the team; that is, startled all but one. One other person heard the rhythmic tapping that night. She too was overtaken by heart-wrenching fear.

We continued navigating around the grave markers, statues, and walls. We found ourselves in the center of the graveyard before we heard the first one, "Thump." The sound of something dropping

The mausoleum at Riverside Cemetery.

was followed by the sound of rolling. We curiously turned around to see nothing but darkness; completely silent. "Thump…" it happened again! This time, we saw an object move. It was a rock. A rock had just been thrown in our direction. "Thump…" a third time. This time, the throw was stronger and the rock came close to us. An intense feeling of danger began to swell within us. We decided to move our investigation back to the front of the cemetery. The rock throwing continued as we made our way back to where we started. Due to the risk of the situation, we decided to end our chilling exploration. It was the first investigation where I heard the clear and distinct voice of a young girl greeting me in such a questioning and worrisome manner. It was also the first night I had heard the mind-bending sound of noises coming from a corpse in a casket. Nothing but a slim, brick wall separated me from *it*…. Lastly, it was the first time I was given such a strong and aggressive message that I was not welcome.

The following day, a team member and I met a mutual friend at "Riverside Cemetery" to tell of the horror film-like experience we had. The cemetery was illuminated by the sun at this point. Yet, as we made our way out of the cemetery, it happened: "Thump…" The three

The time-aged gravestones of Riverside Cemetery.

A section of Riverside Cemetery.

of us turned around to see a rock rolling in our direction. It stopped rolling once it reached and touched the foot of our mutual friend. No one was in the cemetery except the three of us. To say we were speechless is an understatement. Though years have passed, I often wonder who I angered so magnificently that fateful night. I haven't heard that unholy tapping since. However, sometimes as I retire for the night, I can still hear it in my mind, "Tap, scratch, tap, scratch, tap..." It keeps me up for hours. Other times I wonder if a few of the spirits I encountered followed me home that night to remind me of their chilling presence. I don't know, all I know is, I am not the only one who has had such experiences in The Riverside Cemetery. As I tell my story, some people laugh it off as if I merely recall a nightmare created in my mind the night before; others, I can see the fear in their eyes. The difference is: those who have fear possess a shared fear. A fear which those who have encountered the poltergeists at Riverside know all too well...

The Blood-Stained Basement

Benson, Johnston County

No one saw it coming. The entire town was left in morbid discomfort, the man's family, left heart-broken. The chaos brought about from a decision originally planned through good intentions. In his letter, he claimed the cause was financial matters. Alas, this was not the truth. The incident took place in October of the year 1921. Since then, the town has moved on forgetting what happened in the Mary Duncan Library. That is, almost the entire town. A small handful of people, mainly a specific kind of people employed at the library are aware of the man. You see, he thought what he did would be a means of ultimately escaping the torturous reality he created. Only time would show that it wasn't the answer. He has been left, in the exact spot, where he decided to take his own life. Again, the shadow in the basement was largely forgotten, his presence made known only to select library employees over the generations. It is rare when the identity of a ghost is known. This story is one of those rare occasions. Before I reveal any details, I must inform you: out of respect for the family of the man of whom I speak, he will be known only by his first and middle initials "C.B." You are now informed. Shall we continue?

Before the town library's home, the building now named "The Mary Duncan Library" was "Farmer's Commercial Bank." Constructed in 1919, the bank opened in late 1920–early 1921. The bank was successful. So was the insurance business which operated out of one office in a portion of the bank's first floor. The insurance company was operated by Mr. C.B. The gentleman

The Mary Duncan Public Library.

became very successful in his business which enabled him to support his wife and three daughters. A large festival was coming to the small, country town of Benson. There were rides, food, music, and entertainers. C.B. was eager to attend. Perhaps, a little too eager. His decision to attend would be the beginning of his sorrowful end. While at the festival, C.B. found himself unable to peal his eyes from a certain show. Alas, the show itself did not hold the man's gaze. Rather, one of the showgirls. Mr. C.B. became fixated on an attractive, young dancer. She too appeared to single him out of the audience. Despite better judgment, he decided to wait after the show was over in hopes of speaking with her.

The two spoke and their passions became an uncontrollable fire. C.B. and the entertainer spoke and met in secret until the festivities left Benson, taking the lady with them. After she left, C.B. tried to return to his normal life, pushing the unfaithfulness to his wife towards the back of his mind. He was unable to return to his once routine life. Nor would he adapt to any other variation of normality. C.B. underwent countless hours and days of bodily suffrage. While C.B. was with the dancer, he contracted a venereal disease.

As the consequence of his actions became clear, the truth was made publicly known. His guilt and shame, coupled with his daily pains, grew to such an extent that he could not face his wife, children, and fellow men again. Early one morning, C.B. arrived at work. He walked through the bank and into his office. Full of regret, Mr. C.B. ended his life. His remains were found by the bank owner sometime after.

The bank was sold during the Great Depression and was eventually renovated to become the Mary Duncan Library. The office of Mr. C.B. was closed off, as if to seal forever the horrifying memories eternally plastered upon the walls and floors. It is used as nothing more than extra storage space. Since the opening of the library in 1931, apparitions of a man sitting on the basement steps have been observed. The man can also be seen stressfully pacing the basement floors as if he is in agonizing contemplation. The sightings of C.B. do not stop there. Over the years, as women employees enter the basement, they have reported being grabbed by the arms or ankles,

GH. N. C., FRIDAY MORNING, OCTOBER 28, 1921.

War" left for Williamsport. He will be out of the city until about the first week in December.

SUICIDE COMMITTED BY BENSON BUSINESS MAN

C. B. [ ] Shoots Himself Through Head While Sitting In His Office

Benson, Oct. 27.—"I cannot bear the worries and burdens of life any longer." Thus wrote C. B. [ ] of the Benson Loan and Insurance Company, before blowing his brains out in his office in the Farmers Commercial bank building this morning, about six o'clock.

[ ] arose above five o'clock this morning, writing a note to his wife, the contents of which have not been disclosed, before leaving his residence. He then walked down to his office, penned a note to a friend, greeted the janitor of the building, who had already arrived to commence his morning chores, then sat down in an office chair and shot himself twice with a revolver behind the right ear.

Death was not instantaneous the unfortunate man living for about an hour in an unconscious condition after he had committed his rash act. While deceased was known to be in debt for small amounts, his resources were far greater than his liabilities and friends cannot understand why his financial worries should lead him to self-destruction.

COMMISSION ALLOWS ELKIN BANK TO REOPEN

The Corporation Commission has granted permission for the resumption

C.B. suicide notice, *The News and Observer* (October 28, 1921).

The decrepit room believed to be the insurance office of Mr. C.B.

The stairway on which the ghost of C.B. is seen.

The bookshelves where the roaming, female entity is seen.

shoved, and watched. No male employee has experienced such happenings. The ghost is only seen in the basement and will never leave the place wherein he spent his final moments. He thought it was the answer. Now, C.B. exists only in the moment in time that brought him to his untimely death.

Do not feel heavy-hearted, dear reader. At least, not yet... Perhaps the woman with whom C.B. fulfilled his lustful desires received her just deserts as well. A second ghost is known to roam the library. An apparition of a woman with long black hair and a white dress is often seen wandering the library, effortlessly gliding from corner to corner and between bookshelves. She brings with her a sense of being lost or waiting. Any efforts exercised in hopes of discovering for what, or *whom*, she awaits is as good as dead. Only one warning remains regarding this hopelessly lost soul: if you stumble into her presence, do not try to interact with her. For if you do, her torture-like reality will become yours to share.

The Secret Beneath
the Bridge

Mill Creek, Johnston County

Southeastern Johnston County is known for being home to the rough and rugged: people who choose to live in the "true country" and face the forces of nature accompanied by a few like-minded neighbors—if they are lucky. This has always been the case. Except for one individual: a single man, who was as heartless as Hell itself. Though the man lived more than 192 years ago, his mere existence left its mark on history by being the manifestation of "hate." Townspeople and historians alike choose to call him only by his surname. They fear exposing his given name would bring shame and misfortune to his now future descendants. To much astonishment, this man, who is known only as Lynch, is not remembered for his ghastly life. Lynch is remembered for the suffering he was *(and is)* forced to endure once his life came to a bloody end.

In the year 1831, Lynch was a plantation owner. He owned many acres of land on which he grew cotton, tobacco and other cash crops. To work the land were the misfortunate slaves who belonged to the man. Lynch was a cruel master and was known for providing just enough means for his enslaved to barely live. Lynch's slaves were so unkempt and their extreme diet altered their physical appearances. As eyewitness accounts state, all of Lynch's slaves had red hair. This was not the process of genetics. Rather, it was due to the only food they were permitted to eat which consisted of Hayman potatoes and cow tallow. Even though the slaves existed in such incomprehensible conditions, they worked as diligently and faithfully as they could. This was so for many years until

Lynch pushed one slave past his threshold. That day, the hated master learned that everyone has a breaking point.

It was the end of a bitterly cold and trying day filled with endless work and countless beatings. As the sun began to set, Lynch chose one of the largest slaves he had, an aged man known as "Old Squire," to begin work in a cornfield located along the side of Mill Creek. Old Squire was given a metal hoe and began his journey with Lynch. As the two men reached the bridge which crosses over the creek, Old Squire collapsed with exhaustion due to his age and strenuous labor. Outraged by this, Lynch screamed at the poor old man and demanded he rise to his feet. Unwilling to give Squire a chance to muster his strength, Lynch whipped the downed man unmercifully. As Old Squire felt the lashes of the whip opening the skin on his back, and felt his blood causing his shirt to stick to the fresh wounds, he felt something erupt within him. Old Squire did manage to stand that evening. He turned around, raised his heavy hoe above his head and with it penetrated the skull of Lynch with as much force as he had left. Lynch's silenced body collapsed on the wooden bridge with a bone-jarring thud.

Terrified of what consequence awaited Old Squire for killing his master, he dragged Lynch's fresh corpse below the bridge. With his hoe, Squire broke through the frosted ground and buried the body of the man he once called master beside the portion of Mill Creek which runs beneath the bridge. He cleaned the blood and matter from the hoe and proceeded back to the slave quarters. The next morning, Lynch's disappearance was discovered. The slaves, including Old Squire, were tasked in helping find the vanished plantation owner. The freedman searched for Lynch, appearing to be as diligent in his search as everyone else. The investigation eventually ended and Lynch remained missing. Lynch's case ran cold. As time progressed, it became "old news" to the townspeople, except for Old Squire. To him, the cold case transformed into a cold burden, one which he would be forced to carry until his final breath. Sometime after the murder, unexplained things began to occur at the Mill Creek Bridge. These *things* would shift Old Squire's burden to incredible panic as he realized he never actually rid the world of Lynch.

The bridge where Lynch's ghost lingers.

The first of many hauntings on Mill Creek Bridge claimed a traveler as its first victim. A man, who journeyed by foot, was determined to complete his navigation without having to camp through the night. Once the light of day was totally subdued by the glow of the moon, the traveler lit a torch which he fashioned from nearby pine wood. His torch burnt with confidence and fulfilled his visual needs. Keeping pace, the man began to hear the sound of moving water. Shortly after, he found himself quickly approaching a wooden bridge and then set foot upon it. As soon as he felt the change from dirt to wood beneath his feet, his torch extinguished, leaving the poor man engulfed by darkness. Unable to view his surroundings, and unable to relight his torch, the dread-filled traveler walked across the bridge unknowing that a murdered corpse rested just below him. As he reached the end of the bridge, his torch caught fire once more, as if someone relit it from behind him.

Another man fell victim to Lynch's unkind manners. This man—advanced in age—ventured across the bridge for the first (and only) time. He chose to end his long walks many years ago due to requiring a cane to complete any task with which walking was associated. One average day, the old man decided to cross the bridge on foot rather than wait and have someone do his business for him. He placed his cane securely on the wood, which was older than he was, and began his vigilant crossing of the bridge. As he took the next step, he found himself falling to the hard, wooden planks. He peered around him to locate his cane; it was no longer near him, nor did it remain on the bridge at all.

Confused and a bit cross, he was left with no choice but to hoist his battered body upwards to reach the other side of the creek. Grasping whatever he could find to help steady himself, he traversed the bridge. Upon reaching the other side, and in desperate need for rest after his vigorous bridge crossing, he decided to lean against a nearby tree. As the gentleman regained his breath, he felt a touch upon his thigh. Resting on his leg, the one for which his cane was needed, was the cane. In a state of shock, the elderly man raised his gaze from his mysterious cane to his strange surroundings. As he suspected, he remained alone.

A third individual experienced an unexplained phenomenon at the site of the murder. As this person set foot on the damned bridge, he found himself surrounded by the echoing of heavy chains, clinking about as if someone were shaking them in the most aggressive manner. These and many more queer happenings were experienced on Mill Creek Bridge. Yet none has ever been able to match the mortifying encounter experienced by Aaron Lee. Lee was a notable academic who appears to have had some connection with the University of North Carolina at Chapel Hill. This fact is known through the presence of some of his work discovered within the collection of Doctor Ira W. Rose of the School of Pharmacy at Chapel Hill. Aaron was a chemist. Apart from this, Mr. Lee's personal research involved the paranormal. Aaron Lee lived near Mill Creek which gave a way for him to hear these outrageous claims travelers and neighbors alike shared about the nearby bridge.

Aaron Lee grew to be utterly mystified by such claims and wished to provide answers from his reputable scientific perspective. One late autumn evening, Lee decided to ride his horse to the small town of Newton Grove. Considering the wonderful weather, Lee and his horse were in no rush to return home. As time went on, Aaron became conscious of the swift approach of nightfall. Noticing this, and the steep decline of the temperature, Lee and his horse made their way home. Only this time, Lee decided to take a different path, a way which would lead him over the bridge to which much attention, and fear, had been given.

Lee noticed nothing of interest as his horse kept a strong and steady canter. This would all change the moment they came to the vicinity of the bridge. A powerful, ice-cold gust of wind smashed into Lee and his horse. The horse came to a sliding halt. Confused as to why his horse stopped moving, Aaron Lee gently pressed his heels into her sides to signal for the animal to advance. The horse began to move in a noticeably lethargic manner, as if each of its four legs had dreadfully heavy weights attached.

Lee gave as much encouragement to his beloved horse as he but, alas it did not work. The beast continued to struggle as if it carried a load two times heavier than her ability. Aaron became exceedingly worried for his faithful friend. However, Lee's worry would quickly be engulfed by fear, the kind of fear which causes the task of inhaling nearly impossible. A sound came of something large rolling and thudding against the cold, lifeless ground beneath the bridge. It was the disturbing sound of something struggling: uncomfortable noises were quickly met by the sound of a human, a man, gasping for air, only to be succumbed by whatever—or *whomever*—he struggled with. These nightmarish sounds repeated over and over until Lee and his horse reached the very middle of the bridge. At this point, the struggling man beneath the bridge began to say something in a voice that sounded as if it belonged to someone breathing their last, fearful breath, "Squire... Squire... Squire." Almost petrified by fear, Lee clutched the reins and begged his horse to find strength enough to canter once more.

As the two cleared the bridge, the unholy noises dissipated into the night air. Aaron Lee and his horse, who was in desperate need of rest, finally made it home that night. Once Lee dismounted from his horse, the animal galloped, noticeably relieved of its unseen weight. It is said that the horse ran two miles in the direction of the town of Smithfield before returning. Once the horse came back, Aaron Lee noticed that he was drenched in sweat and foam and was unable to be ridden. The poor animal remained in that state for the rest of its life.

As years passed, this experience and the sounds Lee heard haunted him. During the early 1840s, Lee spent much of his off-time speaking to townspeople about the bridge and his encounter with Lynch. The townspeople were intrigued to learn about the strange happenings of the scholarly individual. Yet, one man, an older man, was most interested. As time advanced, so did Aaron and the old man's life. As the unnamed man lay on his deathbed, his final request was for a visit from Aaron Lee. Lee dashed to the house of the man to bid a final farewell. The man had something else in mind, for he wished to explain to Lee his fascination with Lynch's ghost. The man confessed to being once known as Old Squire. He also confessed to the murder of Lynch as well as all the details attached to it. Shortly after his confession, he died.

Aaron Lee was left unable to utter a word. He left the bedside of Old Squire and mourned the loss of a friend. Though he mourned, he shared an unexplainable terror, a terror of realizing that he unknowingly befriended a murderer. Lynch's ghost is still seen to this day and the bridge still seeks victims to fall prey to its evil, ghostly happenings. If there is anything one might take from the retelling of these paranormal activities, let it be this: never venture to the Mill Creek Bridge alone or you may just encounter Hate himself...

The Creaking
of the Gallows

Hannah's Creek Swamp,
Johnston County

The years from 1861 to 1865 are forever fused with anguish, fear, and death in American history. These five, brutal years are sealed by the bloodiest war America has ever seen: the Civil War. So many Americans died during this war between brothers that there simply was not enough time to properly bury each fallen soldier. Countless bodies were left, in the exact spot where they were slain, to rot. This

Hannah's Creek Swamp.

was so common that many of those poor men's names and identities weathered away along with their battered bodies. Considering these facts, it should be no surprise that an uptick in paranormal phenomena was immediately reported following the gruesome fights. In fact, most Civil War battlegrounds hold at least one ghost story. Such is the case with many areas in North Carolina. With roughly 85 battles and engagements fought in the Old North State alone, spotting an apparition of a Union or Confederate soldier in the battlefront state of North Carolina is not merely a possibility, but a likelihood.

During the War, select soldiers on both the Union and Confederate sides banded together to form groups of outlawed men whose only purpose was to pillage, plunder, and destroy anything that still stood after troops passed through towns. Such is the case for a group of Union men who were known as the Marauders. Led by Colonel David Fanning, these men had once been honorable members of the Union who fought to preserve the United States of America. However, they were quickly shamed by the Union Army once they began their actions of ill repute. In 1865, shortly after Northern General William Sherman marched through the town of Smithfield, the Marauders followed, hoping to steal food and goods which had been left for the unarmed townspeople. Not only did the outlaws steal much needed food and goods from the people of Smithfield, they attempted to strike fear into the hearts of the people of Johnston County by raiding the house of a prominent family in the county. After the raid, the Marauders murdered the husband and wife. This action caused a reaction which the outlaws never forgot....

After stealing the lives of the Saunders couple, Fanning and his men fled to the outskirts of town. They found refuge in the swamplands of Hannah Creek. After setting camp, and assuming the townspeople had retired for the night, the group felt safe enough to study some of their newly acquired possessions. This act alone would prove to be a fatal mistake. Among some of the loot taken from the Saunders estate was a medium-size, oaken jewelry box. Fanning quietly and cautiously opened the heirloom box. Inside was stored gold, pearl, and ivory jewelry and accessories. One item caught the attention of David; it was a pendant in the shape of a cross. The gold of the necklace shone in the light of the moon; the artistic detail proclaimed the purity which belonged to the former and rightful owner of the piece. As Fanning admired the cross, the sound of distant footsteps slushing through the swamp broke the stillness of the night.

The bounty inspection was cut short by the arrival of a troop of Confederate men. As soon as the Marauders left the murder scene, townsfolk rushed to the Confederate colonel who was stationed in Smithfield at the time of the raid. The colonel, a Mr. John Saunders, was outraged at hearing of such shameful acts. Alas, his outrage was soon replaced by a strange and unimaginable mixture of pain and anger as the townspeople directed him to the elderly couple's home. The people unknowingly guided him to his childhood home, the home which had so unexpectedly become the crime scene. At that moment, Colonel Saunders rallied his men and promised to find the men who killed his parents.

As Colonel Saunders approached David Fanning and his men, he noticed a small but beautiful cross dangling from Fanning's clinched fist. The pendant hung between the knuckles of the murderer as its chain hid within David's hand which rested against his thigh as he slowly backed away from the Confederate men. Saunders bypassed all questions of interrogation and ordered for each man to be executed at once. Holding Fanning at gunpoint, he was forced to watch each of his men choke their final breaths as they were hanged in the swamp. When it was time for David Fanning to receive his death penalty, Colonel Saunders wished to carry out the task himself.

Each body was left in the swamp at Hannah's Creek to stand as a warning for anyone who might wish so much as to ponder such foul acts and to ensure the total decomposition of the integrity of each of the fifty men. When questioned on how he knew that these men committed the murder, Colonel John Saunders referred to the cross he spotted in David Fanning's hand—a gift he had bought for his mother.

Not only was Hannah's Creek given the unwanted seal of bloodshed and death, but it was also bequeathed with the souls of those fifty heinous men. Since the end of the war, locals and visitors alike witness strange and utterly disturbing sounds and apparitions in the swamp of Hannah's Creek. Sounds of men gargling and gasping for

The small island located in Hannah's Creek Swamp.

air are heard; the unmistakable tight creaking of suspended rope, grasping a heavy object, slowly swaying in the wind is also reported. However, the most common mystery held by the swamplands—and most terrifying—is that of the apparitions. The chilling outline of bodies hanging from the trees are regularly seen. Almost as if the men still stand—or perhaps *dangle*—as an ever-present warning for anyone contemplating such hateful crimes.

Though the Civil War ended and the dispute settled many years ago, it appears some restless souls wish to carry out the duties they never brought to fruition. Perhaps, the souls of the lost soldiers roam the battlegrounds and final resting places in hopes of some-how, sometime, reattaching their names and stories to their bodies. What if some souls are left to relive their final moments of suffrage for eternity as in the case of the souls at Hannah's Creek? To choose one hypothesis to explain the presence of Civil War paranormali-ties would be wrong. There is but one bit of advice to retain: cling tightly to your cross pendant when you journey near the swamplands at Hannah's Creek.

The Unseen Bystanders

Bentonville, Johnston County

There exists a phenomenon within the realm of the paranormal which baffles both scientists and mystics alike: a "supernatural crossing of times," if you will. In other words, this strange yet regularly experienced occurrence can be briefly defined as a "paranormal time loop" wherein fully intact scenes from the past visit the present. Science attempts to explain this experience through the psychological theory of involuntary recurrent memory—the sudden but powerful re-experiencing of a past experience. Mystics claim that only certain individuals, such as empaths, can experience these happenings through a shared sensitivity to the spiritual reality. Perhaps the causation for such bizarre encounters is due to the exact replication of atmospheric conditions.

Whatever the case may be, these outrageous claims manage to capture both the psyches and emotions of people all over the globe, often leaving fear branded in the minds and hearts of those lucky— or *unlucky*—enough to share in this unfathomable variation of accidental time travel.

One such encounter is that of Jim Weaver and his hunting partner, Joe Lewis, of Bentonville Township when they experienced a Civil War battle which took place forty years after the war concluded. It was an unexpected eyewitness account of the undead battle of Bentonville. The year was 1905. Jim Weaver was a native of the Bentonville area. He was known as an eccentric. His hair was long and unkempt, which matched his scraggly beard. His clothing consisted of rags held together by his own stitch work, which was sloppy at best. He never wore shoes. Needless to say, Mr. Weaver fully embraced the woodsman identity. One thing was known of the man: he was an enthusiastic hunter. His favorite game was possum.

Joe Lewis was an Englishman who carried himself in a manner much different from, perhaps completely opposite to, Jim. However, the two found common ground through their shared passion for hunting. They were known to hunt regularly, at least once a week. This would all change after one fateful night. It was normal for them to carry extra equipment to fend off bobcats or coyotes but no amount of weaponry could prepare them for the trauma they were about to experience.

The duo began their hunt at early nightfall. Jim and Joe began by tracking possums on foot. It was a normal Saturday in March. They spent hours following the trail of a few possums deep into the woods. The team found themselves in the old trenches and other manmade structures left by the War of the Rebellion. By the position of the moon, Weaver knew it was past midnight. However, the two decided to press onward as they knew they were closing in on a large possum. Jim silently led the way, using the trench walls as a guide. The slow and steady crunching of leaves and twigs beneath their feet broke the silence of the night. The trail led them to the base of a small but sturdy tree up which the possum had fled. Filled with excitement that their diligent and tedious work had come to a climax, Jim took a small ax from his haversack and prepared to chop down the tree. Widening his stance until his feet were the same width as his shoulders and drawing his arm back to gain as much momentum as he could, Weaver delivered a hearty blow to the soft pine tree. To Jim's surprise, he received a response for which he could never have prepared.

As the blade of the ax penetrated the bark of the tree, Jim felt a teeth-shattering shock, as if his ax made contact with iron, leaving him unprepared to brace for such an impact. At that exact moment, he saw a flash of light illuminate the nearby tree line for a brief second, only to be followed by another unexplainable illumination. The flashes of light were soon accompanied by the deafening sound of explosions. From a distance, he heard a faint sound which grew to the unmistakable roar of screaming men. The silent hunt had morphed into a nightmarish battle that erupted from thin air. Jim's heart-bursting fear made it impossible for him to run.

Weaver too stood victim to the horrors of war. Without notice, and with the screams approaching his vicinity, he saw men, some wearing blue pants and white shirts, others wearing fully decorated Union uniforms dashing to and fro, finding refuge behind surrounding trees. Seconds later, from the opposite side, he observed men in gray, running and galloping on horseback in the direction of the Union soldiers; all demonstrating the famed "Rebel yell." As the two sides clashed, gunfire from 19th-century rifles filled the area in which Jim stood. Jim reluctantly became witness to the killing and dying of men in the most gruesome of manners. As if Weaver's unfathomable reality was not enough, his nightmare increased as hand-to-hand combat took place.

In the midst of men screaming for their lives as they fought and died unspeakable deaths, arose a flag bearer. A young, Confederate man forced himself past comrade and enemy alike as he tightly held his regiment's flag. The young man, perhaps even boy, was

One of the existing trenches at Bentonville.

met by a Union soldier. The two clashed in an unforgettable quarrel. The Union soldier heroically grabbed the pole on which the Confederate's flag swayed and began disarming the soldier. As the Union man nearly accomplished his task, a second rebel rushed to aid his man. As the third man assisted the flag bearer, the feud gained attention by nearby soldiers. The assisting Confederate soldier was stopped by a Union bullet; his body crashed onto the dirt in a way similar to a tree cut from its base. The flag bearer released a voice-cracking scream filled with both fear and anger.

With the death of his fellow Confederate, the Union aggressor took the opportunity to seize his bayonet and stab the second Confederate. His blade penetrated through the upper portion of the young man's arm. Using his bayonet, the Union soldier forced the Confederate man to the ground, pinning him and with a strong, full-body turn, faced the direction in which Jim Weaver stood. The pale hunter saw the blood-smeared face of the warrior. The Union man's blue eyes and clenched teeth appeared as if he could see Jim; his posture seemed as if he was prepared to lunge towards Weaver.

At this sight, Jim managed to break his effigy-like state and muster enough courage to move. The hunters managed to run out of the wooded trenches. Their hearts filled with adrenaline; their legs were numbed by fear. As they ran further from the battle, the sounds ceased, as well as the flashes of the artillery. Weaver and Lewis ran in the direction of the Harper House. But because they saw an unusual light through the windows of the home, coupled with the experience they had just escaped, they did not dare attempt to seek haven within its walls. The exhausted and anxiety ridden hunters did not stop their running until they arrived at the house of Mr. Weaver. The two men lived in a state of anxiety easily triggered by sudden and loud noises until their dying days.

The two men proclaimed their *ghostly attack* to hundreds of locals and visitors. It was not uncommon for the response to such a tale to be that of silence. What does one do when presented with such claims? The most outrageous variable of the present experience is that of its accuracy. On March 19, 1865, an unimaginably gruesome battle took place in the trenches and earthworks of Bentonville.

It was on that day that a certain Confederate, Joseph Johnston, aimed to prevent 60,000 of Union General Sherman's men from joining forces with General Ulysses S. Grant. The battle claimed not only thousands of lives but also continued until the 21st of March. The battle faded with the echoes of cannon fire late into the night of the 21st. Not only were Weaver and Lewis honest men, but history adds validity to their deathly claims.

Afterward the eyewitness Jim Weaver joined Smithfield's group of Confederate Veterans in an effort to learn more about the very battle he observed. Naturally, he told the men of his encounter. As Weaver concluded his recollection of the Battle of Bentonville, an awkward silence filled the room. The men had mixed expressions as they pondered the decision to believe the man or not. That is, all but one man who knew without a doubt that Weaver's story was authentic. He was merely 17 years old those 40 years ago. The man served as flag bearer for his unit. His left arm was maimed due to a bayonet stab he suffered while attempting to carry his flag through the Battle of Bentonville. The movement of his left arm was not the only thing the man lost that night. His brother was slain as he attempted to help him defend their flag.

Though the bone-chilling, eyewitness account of Jim Weaver took place more than 100 years ago, it remains terrifying today. As for the mysterious lights shining from the windows of the Harper House, this too can be understood through historical context: the Harper House was used as a field hospital during the three-day-long battle. The souls of dead Civil War soldiers are still seen and heard as they linger within the trenches and Harper House, awaiting the final stand-off. Perhaps they are trapped due to their agonizing and sudden demise.

Visitors claim to see soldiers, some standing, others patrolling, in the woods surrounding the earthworks and within the surviving trenches. Sounds of gunshots and screams are also regularly occurring aspects of the battlefield. However, the most common location on the Bentonville battlegrounds for paranormal activity is the Harper House itself. Faces and victims of war are often observed in the windows of the field hospital. Likewise, the

The Harper House.

blood-curdling cries of the dying are heard, leaving visitors deeply disturbed. If you visit the battlegrounds at Bentonville, you'd be smart to prepare yourself for an unexpected taste of the bloodiest war in American history.

I Live in a Haunted House

Benson, Johnston County

"Sometimes I don't believe what happens to me because it seems so far-fetched but, I assure you, it's all true." These are the opening remarks of Mr. Shane Booth; a 45-year-old professor of photography who yearned to own and live in a historic house. Mr. Booth quickly discovered that he received more than he bargained for—much more. The professor is known for being a very upbeat individual. Students and fellow faculty of the local college know him for the charming manner in which he carries himself, his relaxed personality, and his lecturing style. Students might even consider

The haunted house of Shane Booth.

Booth to be a "friend-like" instructor with a rather optimistic outlook on life.

Little did anyone know, Professor Booth lived a second reality—an existence riddled with radiating fear and terror, plagued with hauntings and paranormal attacks. It was a life which no level of familiarity with academia could ever explain. Booth's outlandish accounts are so terrifying that they were included in a 2022 issue of *The New York Times* as well as featured in countless paranormal television shows. After reading of the heart-palpitating encounters of Professor Booth, one might think twice when looking to purchase a historic home...

"I chose Benson due to its closeness to the college, and for the one-of-a-kind home I found," Shane Booth goes on to explain, "I've always wanted to live in a historic home. When I saw this one, I instantly fell in love with it." The house of which Mr. Booth speaks is a beautiful abode located in Benson's charming downtown. The house itself was built between 1887 and 1888 and served as the first church in the town, the Benson Baptist Church. As time continued, the church was moved from its original plot to its current one and the original building was converted into a private residence in 1913. This information remained unknown to Shane Booth until his research revealed it later. According to him:

"As I walked within the house, I glanced at the unique shape of the ceiling. It is an arch-shaped ceiling, similar to a church steeple. I continued walking through the empty home and noticed something strange in one of the back rooms. There was writing on the walls. The writing was scribbled, almost like a child had gotten ahold of a pen. The most peculiar part about it was that the poor penmanship was of names and depictions of scenes. As curiosity prompted, I began to research the names etched into the centuries-old walls. I discovered that the home I had just purchased was originally a church! Knowing this, I would have never expected to experience the things I have, and continue to encounter, in my house.

"As soon as I moved in, I instantly noted strange things; residual things: the sound of tapping on the walls, footsteps on the hardwood floors, and the sudden, soft whispers of another person in the house. At first, I thought nothing of these sounds. Perhaps the floor was settling in unusual ways due to the structure's being more than 135 years old. The vocalized sounds were nothing more than small gusts of wind which found a way through unseen cracks ... or so I thought. I must admit, the first unexplainable phenomenon was very unusual. One morning, as I opened my front door to begin my errands, I noticed a pile of seashells neatly placed in the middle of my porch. Benson is nowhere near the ocean. Numerous questions entered my mind as I stood in the doorway utterly confused. Being new to the town, I decided my best bet was to question my neighbors as to why seashells were on my porch."

Benson's first church, now the haunted residence of Shane Booth.

As Mr. Booth stood on his porch, straining to articulate a reason for the seashells, he beckoned fellow neighbors and passersby, "Excuse me, I'm new here and, I know this is going to sound a bit odd but, I walked onto my front porch this morning to find an unusual pile of seashells, neatly placed in the middle of my porch. Do you happen to know who they belong to or how they got there?" Each time he asked, he received the same answer: silence. It seemed his neighbors wished to be left alone by Mr. Booth—or left alone by *something else...*

"Having no answer, I brushed off the unusual gift—if you want to call it that—and carried on my way. In the days to follow, I experienced a few odd things. I heard the sounds of boots walking across my hardwood floor at nights, I saw random flashes of light, rhythmic knocking on walls, and I've even heard people talking. Somehow, I managed to cough up some excuse for everything. Maybe this was the wrong thing to do because, whatever was in my house didn't like to be ignored... Everything changed one night in a way I never saw coming."

Before I continue to record the hauntings, I must first relay this: the Professor made it rather clear to me the deep and unbreakable love and care he has and expresses to his animals. He is the proud owner of Matilda, a 60-pound boxer/dalmatian mix and, at the time, Lana who was a Great Dane weighing 145 pounds. As you will soon understand, the information expounded serves as crucial variables to Mr. Booth's encounters.

The Violent Poltergeist

"I folded into the comfort of my living room couch. After a day full of work and activities, I wanted to just relax and watch a bit of TV. My dog, Matilda, was curled on the floor and sleeping in such a way that even glancing at her would cause drowsiness to gently blow over the observer. All was indeed calm. As I gazed upon the screen of my television, I noticed small movements, shivers, coming from the floor. It was Matilda; she was shaking. Her shaking became jolts as they grew in intensity. My heart began to pound as I felt the shock of adrenaline and fear course through my body. My initial thought was, 'She is having a seizure.' I leaped from my resting position and threw myself over her. I hugged her and spoke calming words to her as her body, now held in my arms, continued to thrash. My embrace seemed to work and she eventually returned to a state of conscious awareness.

"Matilda's convulsive state was utterly horrendous to watch. It seemed clear to me that it was a seizure. There was still a sliver of doubt in my mind that it was a true seizure. You see, when she began shaking, it mirrored the same motions as a dog experiencing a panic attack. It was almost as if she saw an abuser approaching her and she knew her impending fate and fear took over. It broke my heart. I decided to take her outside to help her as best I could. I watched her closely as I grabbed her leash from its placement by the door. As gently as I could, I attached the leash to her collar and slowly began to walk her to the front door. I did not take my eyes off her which is exactly why I know it wasn't a seizure. She did see something and my 'sliver of doubt' showed to be the traumatizing truth. She took but a few steps before she was thrust into the air as if someone had kicked her in the side as hard as humanly possible. I will never forget the sound she let out. The air was forced out from her. Air refilled her lungs only to be thrust out again with a painful yelp. Once she landed, the violent shaking returned."

Shane threw himself upon his best friend once again to protect her from an unseen, attacking force. Once she was shrouded in Shane's embrace, she felt safe enough to relax once again. The attack did not reoccur. No, the poltergeist achieved its goal of sending its message (even in such a disgusting manner). It—whoever *"it"* was— was not to be ignored. The next day, Mr. Booth took Matilda to the vet and retold the puzzling account. After conducting a series of tests, the doctors concluded that Matilda had not suffered a seizure.

Desperate for Attention

It is often said that the reasoning for residual hauntings is due to a lost soul's need to share a message or perhaps wish to be "known" in some deathly sense. If this be true, how far are the paranormal ready to go to gain such attention from the living? After reading Professor Booth's next account, you will probably agree with me when I say there exists no limit as to how far the dead will venture if they desperately want one's attention.

"When we returned from the vet, I began to entertain the idea of a possible haunting. The strange sounds and otherworldly echoes had not stopped and there remains absolutely no logical nor medical explanation for what Matilda experienced and I witnessed that night. I entered a state of being 'on-edge' for a while after the incident. As time would show, my hesitating manner both served its purpose and only worsened.

"The day was like any other day. It was the weekend so I wasn't at the college. I finally had time to do everyone's favorite activity ... laundry. I brought my basket of clean clothes to my bed and began the task of folding each piece and placing it in its proper stack before returning it to the dresser drawers once again. It was a clear day outside, as far as the weather was concerned, and Matilda was carrying on in her dog ways as she roamed from room to room, the sound of her nails clicking against the antique wood was the only audible aspect of the day. As I said, it was a totally normal day. Then, the unmistakable sound of thick glass shattering from a forceful impact broke the 'normality' of the day. 'CRASH!' Without missing a beat, I dropped the button-up on my bed and dashed in the direction of the sound. What I saw left me deeply afraid."

"Beside my front door are two matching small windows placed on opposite sides of the upper corners of the door. One of the windows no longer matched, as the glass was missing. I looked around and thought it was strange that Matilda had not run to investigate the sound. I found it doubly strange that there was no glass littering the aged floors. Naturally, I peered from the hole where a window once was, to inspect the scene. Not only did I find that all of the glass was on the outside of my house, but so was Matilda! The glass lay roughly twelve feet from the window and Matilda sat directly on the porch, dazed and confused. As I realized the only way Matilda could have gotten outside, my blood ran cold."

The only logical explanation for the crashing obliteration of the window's glass, the direction in which the shattered, razor-like pieces fell, and Matilda being outside, was that, somehow, the 60-pound boxer mix was lifted and thrown through the window. Once the undone professor ushered Matilda back inside, he worrisomely dragged himself back to his bedroom. He was met by the neatly categorized clothes thrown about his room. Insult to injury at its finest. At this moment, I take the pleasant opportunity to inform the reader that though Matilda was left dazed, she was not injured. It seemed that the ghosts which plague the professor's home continued to communicate with him through his animals, a pathway for supernatural communication which *was* practically unheard of.

As Mr. Booth retold these unusual forms of hauntings, a sense of hesitation married with the intense weight of fear could be undoubtedly heard as they seemed to jokingly dance with poor Shane's voice. It seemed to come in bouts, perhaps when a traumatic memory of a hellish encounter was reluctantly pulled from his subconscious into his conscious. Then the heavy load was discarded, as if the memory returned to its unwelcomed place. As you read what Mr. Booth describes next, do not attempt to "pick up" such a weight!

"The Scariest Thing to Ever Happen to Me"—Shane Booth

"I'll never forget this for as long as I live. As I look back on this, there is no 'positive way' to view it. It happened in the middle of the night. I've had a full day so, when night came, I knew I would be sleeping like a dog. As I expected, I crawled into bed (merely making it onto the mattress due to how tired I was). I remained alert long enough to notice both Matilda and Lana leap into the bed, then fell asleep as quickly as a boulder falls off a cliff. I don't know what time it was. It was late—it was really late. Something woke me. I felt a noticeably strange sensation about my feet. As soon as I pried my eyes open, I saw that the foot of my antique iron bed frame was not touching the ground. It was levitating roughly two feet off the ground! I was instantly afraid. Since something unseen was lifting my bed up—thus lifting me—I felt like I was completely vulnerable, left at the mercy of whatever evil *thing* shared my house. As quickly as the bed flew into the air it returned to the ground with a great force. As soon as it jarringly slammed down, Lana, my 145-pound Great Dane, crashed onto the floor. As soon as Lana's giant body thudded on the wood, as if commanded, Matilda lunged in her direction and began viciously attacking her.

"In a manic-like state of fear, anger, and panic, I began screaming at Matilda to cease her unprovoked attack as I bawled my eyes

115

out at the sight of the unadulterated horror. It was no use. Matilda, the 60-pound, oversized lapdog, managed to somehow dominate and inflict wounds on the dog twice her size. Lana's blood began to adorn the walls and floor as I grabbed Matilda and threw my body to the floor in hopes of prying her from her aggression. She eventually halted her cruel actions within a second ... as if commanded. The second she stopped, she very calmly, and very slowly, paced to the middle of my bedroom and sat, staring at us. She did this for ten minutes. Her posture was no longer aggressive while she locked her eyes on us. After the allotted time, she pranced back into bed and curled up for a restful sleep as if nothing happened."

Matilda had never conducted herself in an aggressive manner, nor did she ever act in such a vicious fashion after this incident. Professor Booth believes she was possessed by the dark, unwanted "being" who refuses to leave his abode. After this panic-filled moment, Booth knew he had to do something.

"As soon as I arrived on campus the following day, I told my students about this. I was desperate to talk to someone and was curious

Shane Booth's bedroom where Matilda (shown) was possessed.

to discover if anyone has heard of something like this happening. My students were unable to provide any feedback; it was the first they had heard about it too. However, after my lecture, one student approached me with a bottle of liquid and told me to recite something he wrote on a small piece of paper. He claimed it would make anything evil leave. I didn't understand it (I still don't fully understand it) but I did it, hoping that something would change. After I arrived back home from the college, I stood in my dining room. Facing the table, I opened the small bottle and recited the words he instructed me to say aloud. As I trickled the water, a black figure appeared. It was in the corner of the room. I glanced at the male-shaped apparition and witnessed it morph into a smaller figure, perhaps an animal, and jet, as a beam of light, in the direction of under the table. Almost like it tried to hide."

What was the liquid in the bottle and what were the words given to Shane? I like to think it might have been holy water and a prayer. The true identity of the weapons of defense remains shrouded in mystery. All that is known is that the gruesomely terrible,

Benson's first church converted into a home.

of my grandmother wearing a fur coat. The frame was cracked as if it felt some level of impact once hitting the floor. Yet, it was neatly placed in the center of the room. The most absurd variable is not that it was neatly placed with broken glass remaining on grandmother's photograph, it was that which appeared on the photo under the slivers of glass. Teeth imprints are now part of her picture.

"One of the 'stranger' things to happen was the chicken bones. I had just finished mopping the foyer. After getting to the end, I walked backwards, retracing my steps, to ensure no footprints would blemish my newly cleaned floor. Once I successfully exited the now spotless area, I left my home to go to the store. Once I returned, I unlocked the front door and entered my house. As I walked in, I noticed an object lying in the middle of my cleaned floor. I glanced at it only to discover that chicken bones were mysteriously lying in the exact section I had just cleaned. I was extraordinarily puzzled. I saw no explanation for this, so I just picked them up and threw them away, never to think of them again."

It is true that Professor Booth allowed the "chicken bone incident" to escape his mind ... only to remember it two years later when the exact bones were found lying in the center of one of his doorways. When asked his thoughts about his *haunted reality* he quite honestly answered, "Things like this happen all the time. Most of them are unexplainable. You just kind of get used to all the things you hear around here."

As many stories as there are in this collection, there are simply too many to record in this book alone. Strange things continue to plague the professor: tapping on the walls, voices calling to him, his animals appearing to see things unseen to him. He has seen the apparition of both a man and a woman. He states that they both appear in attire customary to the mid–20th century. However, these two full-body apparitions do not linger for long. As time continued, Booth was lucky enough to become acquainted with a local who was willing to comment on the historic home, a lady who worked in the home years ago. Upon learning he was the lucky—or misfortunate—one to purchase the house, she only had one question: "Do you think it's haunted too?"

Dorothea Dix
Mental Hospital

Raleigh, Wake County

Once upon Dorothea Dix Hill in Raleigh, North Carolina, stood the Dorothea Dix Psychiatric Hospital. The mental ward was opened in the year 1856, more than 167 years ago as I write, and existed as North Carolina's first mental hospital. In the early years, those on the outside noted only the appearance of the mysterious asylum. Throughout the 19th century, and into the first half of the 20th, an undeniable stigma surrounded the topic of mental illness. The sad reality is society deemed a family as vexed

The disturbing placement of the Dix Hill State Hospital stone.

if one of its members was mentally ill. Therefore, those beyond the walls of the gloomy and unapproachable asylum dared not venture nearby. This allowed the hospital to remain largely unrevealed—until now.

The large, tan-colored building adorns the top of Dorothea Dix Hill, giving a mountainous illusion to the single hillside. The cement walls (so solid not even the attack of a war machine could disturb them) are one color: a bleak, yellowish-tan. The dull coloration of the building is broken only by the uncomfortable site of "safe windows"; windows consisting of bullet-proof glass and steel bars to halt any escape plans possibly fashioned by the psychotic. Some might even say, during the early years, that patients of the mental hospital would rather take their chances of jumping, and most assuredly meeting death along with the ground, than stay in the hospital. Why is this, one might ask? Allow me to begin with some of the foul practices of psychological intervention during the 19th century:

Psychology was a new science during the 1800s. Therefore, many of the "treatments" of mentally ill patients were better understood as "experiments." Today, many of the measures taken by psychologists of the past are deemed unethical and remain out of use. Nevertheless, the torture-like treatments that psychotic individuals underwent during these experimental years of the practice were irreversible. One such method was known as the "Utica Crib." To treat patients who were restless (perhaps a patient with schizophrenia experiencing a hallucination) they were forced into a coffin-like space with their hands, feet, arms, legs, and even head strapped to the bottom of the box. A lid was then placed over the box, completely closing and isolating the patient.

Though the box consisted of bars through which the patient could be observed, it undoubtedly transformed the agonizing experience of schizoid-hallucinations into a living hell wherein the sick mind could fully engulf the person's body and soul as he or she lay in an isolated prison cell. Alas, the "treatments" do not stop here. A common practice to treat patients during a manic episode was to forcefully submerge them in a bath of ice water until the episode

The abandoned Dorothea Dix Mental Hospital.

ceased and the patient relaxed—or went limp. Other means of treatments were purging, bloodletting, forcing patients to be in a near endless drug-like state, straitjackets, and lobotomies. For fear that the reader might not finish the rest of this story, I will not go into detail about the other listed methods once thought to relieve mental illness.

Now that one understands a small glimpse of the common practices and horrifying realities many "deranged" individuals knew as everyday life, it should not come as a shock to hear of the hauntings in mental hospitals. Dorothea Dix is no exception. The outside remained shrouded in mystery by those too fearful to enter her intimidating walls. For many years the hauntings at Dorothea Dix Mental Hospital remained silenced, shared only by those brave enough to tour and take up positions at the asylum. Many of the apparitions and ghostly sightings are believed to be past employees and patients alike. Perhaps the patients wish to be known and perhaps search for a peaceful existence, one for which they have always longed—an existence which may never come.

The Night Shift

It was not entirely uncommon to hear patients erupt in nonsensical screams or uncontrollable laughter. At times, the screams and laughter were chucked up to the patients' mental disorders. One past employee states, "Dix was a tough place. Only the uncontrollable were placed there. Some people were suicidal; others were clinically insane; but, the most daunting scenario was that of those placed at the asylum after committing a heinous crime, awaiting a psychiatric evaluation ... those patients usually remained quiet and still. Nothing could wipe that 'blank expression' from their faces."

The hospital was a tough place indeed. Employee turnover was an issue. As another former employee states, "Not everyone was cut out to work there...." However, there existed a core force in the hospital, a group of employees who experienced 15 years or more working with the societal outcasts. When screams and laughter were heard those veteran technicians and staff members questioned the source of the outbursts. Was it due to the patients' mental state or was there *something else* at play. It was easy to assume the first to explain the startling, sometimes sinister, noises but, after seeing what countless staff members and patients witness over the years, so is the latter.

There was never a time at Dix that constituted as "normal." There was always a level of watchfulness which filled the air. Staff diligently watched high-risk patients, waiting to intervene when these poor souls reached (another) breaking point and attempted their, what they thought to be, last-ditch-effort to relieve their pain. Other employees watched themselves and fellow colleagues as it was common for certain residents to attack the staff, hoping to gift them with an incomprehensible, fatal wound. This was merely the day shift. Perhaps the night-shift would be less intense; perhaps, since many of the patients retired for the night, there would be less of a need for such outrageous watchfulness, giving employees a chance to breathe and even the ability to walk the large, echoing halls of the hospital with some level of peace—or so you might think.

Yes, the truth is: many patients did indeed sleep. However, some insisted on denying the body's natural need for rest and stayed alert. As technicians walked through their designated zones and hallways, insuring patients were contained properly in their cells, the halls filled with the quick sound of their hospital-grade shoes knocking on the cold, cement floors and the constant jingle of hospital keychains which served as means for entrance had the staff needed to make an emergency entry into a patient's room. These natural sounds were not the only things to fill the halls of the ward. Every so often, as the technicians made their way through the center of the dimly lit hallways, unnatural laughter (sometimes muffled, other times outbursts) cracked open the normality of the audible aspects of the night shift. The chilling part about the crazed laughing was that it did not mimic the laughter observed in one experiencing hallucinations or manic episodes. It always seemed to be in *response to something.*

Alas, there is something more fearful than the sometimes-sinister laughing which bounced off the walls at Dix. The subtle pleading of patients could be heard. They did not plea to leave the macabre location, rather to stop being *visited,* "Please, I beg you. Leave me alone. I don't want to hear it. I don't want to look." The laughter and pleas echoed from wall to wall as if the building was constructed in such an acoustic manner to purposely force the disturbing and bone-chilling sounds into the ears of those walking, alone, throughout the halls. The mental hospital's soundtrack was enough to cause hair to stand on end and force the individual to second-guess, completing their walk to the end of the morgue-like hallways. The night shift workers of Dorothea Dix were a brave bunch and pushed onward through their routine checks. Most of the time...

As the mental health technicians reached the midway point of the elongated corridors, they, being the only person in each section not in a cell, instantly noted when *another presence* shared the emptiness of the hallways. The night shift, being past visiting hours, knew that they were to be the only people walking the hallways. Thus, the heightened sense of not being alone meant that something was wrong. Once this evolutionary instinct became aroused, staff members took a deep breath and unsuccessfully tried to relax. "It's just because this place is creepy," they often told themselves.

For a brief moment, their grounding strategy triggered relaxation, only to be interrupted by a single skipping of the heart and a flood of numbing adrenaline when they saw *her*. As they approached the ends of their designated hallways, right before the end of the hall intersected with another avenue, a woman, dressed in late 18th-century nursing attire, abruptly turned the corner standing between staff and their exit. The woman always appeared agitated. Her facial and body posture showed cold lifelessness and uncontrollable fury. One's only option was to turn around and begin walking back toward where they originally came from, through the never ending, spine-rattling hallway, leaving the apparition behind them, out of sight... Some employees stood in her presence, unable to move, frozen in fear. Others turned and ran. The apparition never touched an employee. Rather, she utilized her mere presence to eternally scar those who had seen her. Those who chose to run claim that this "nurse-in-death" followed them through the hallway before vanishing altogether.

Through the longstanding time of Dorothea Dix Mental Hospital, the ghost has been seen by thousands and even viewed on surveillance monitors in the nurses' quarters. Who is this mysterious woman and why is she there? Perhaps a more difficult question might be: what has angered her so (in her life or the next)? Over the generations of night shift employees, the identity of the female apparition is claimed to be the famed Dorothea Dix herself, though I do not agree with this. Perhaps the mysterious nurse of death is a former employee of Dix who witnessed the agonizing treatment of the mentally ill those many years ago and, just as in life, wished to help the poor souls who still linger on the forgotten grounds. Perhaps she is angry because the clinically insane were stripped of any hopes for a normal life, including their humanity. Perhaps she is eternally furious because she knows the "peaceful existence" for which they long will indeed never arrive.

Entering the Crypt

The strange and terrifying doors of the insane asylum closed in 2012. Alas, this permanent closing does not keep the spirits from interacting with modern-day visitors. Throughout the lifespan of Dix, thousands of patients never saw the outer walls, and freedom, again. Their—sometimes untimely—deaths occurred within the hospital walls. Sadly, due to the stigma of the time, many bodies of former patients were not collected by their families. This left the hospital with the eerie task of burying its dead. Since the burials were carried out by the hospital, not much went into placing the deceased to rest with their identities intact. In fact, if you venture to (what is now called) "Dorothea Dix Park" you can visit the cemetery. If you do plan a trip, you'll notice a very uncomfortable reality of the cemetery. In the place of full names, and birth and death dates, etched upon the grave markers of many entombed within the cemetery is a singular name (perhaps even nickname). Some bear nothing more than a year. With no families to gather them and with no names left for us (the

Above and following page: **Two examples of the forgotten bodies entombed at the Dorothea Dix Hospital Cemetery.**

living), the authentic identities of each of these poor souls are truly lost. With such depressing lives and equally depressing endings, the cemetery at Dorothea Dix Park stands as one of—if not the most—haunted location in all of Wake County. It seems that the spirits of those interned therein have very reasonable *unfinished business*.

Thanks to the dark and mysterious history at Dorothea Dix Mental Hospital, many paranormal investigators hypothesize that (though the hospital is closed) given the horrifying treatments once administered to many inmates of old, the souls of disturbed patients must linger even to this day. There is but one way to transform such a hypothesis to theory. Every year, thousands of brave investigators from around the country make a once-in-a-lifetime pilgrimage to the cemetery at the unsettling site. Once the sun diminishes and the still of the night engulfs the celestial space, ghost hunters nervously enter the area reserved for the dead and carefully ready their equipment. Everything is conducted with precision and reverence; they are all well aware that this location is reserved for experienced investigators only.

Hunters bring with them into the cemetery "trigger objects" which are special toys, trinkets, and other time-period related things which would be easily recognizable (and hopefully enticing) to the soul of a deceased individual. Balls, easily rolled by the slightest nudge, and small pieces for an otherworldly game of jacks are used to sometimes communicate with younger spirits; an ink quill and paper for spirits who died later in life. Once paranormal investigators tediously place their trigger objects upon the graves chosen, they set their stationary recording cameras in such a manner aiming them at the objects. Leaving the cameras recording, and after taking a much-needed deep breath, they venture deeper into the darkness and to more notoriously haunted spots in the cemetery.

"Hello, I just want to talk to you. Can you tell me your name? Why did they think you were crazy? How did you die?" The investigators allow questions to flow into the night air as they open EVP (Electronic Voice Phenomena) sessions. Not long after, they begin to receive answers. Small noises at first followed by more undeniably human noises. The investigations begin to pick up as they continue navigating through the open space and continue speaking to *whatever* might be following them. As they circle back to their original post, wherein they have strategically placed the trigger objects, they notice the objects' placements have been altered.

In a rush of enthusiasm, they activate their EMF readers (Electromagnetic Field), which indicates even the slightest variation in the surrounding area's electromagnetic field. Hearts begin to pound as the indication needle twitches between medium to high levels of disruptions. Other team members fetch their thermal imaging cameras which allow them to spot any source of body heat unable to be seen with the naked eye. As they activate their thermal cameras, they notice the shades of yellow, blue, and even red figures throughout the graveyard. All are identifying sources of heat in spaces unoccupied by living entities; all are heat signals appearing to be in the shape of people.

The investigators continue until the activity slows and eventually dissipates (or, until their batteries are drained). Before concluding the hunt, they snap a few photographs of the darkened cemetery. For a split second, as the cameras expose the headstones, perhaps there is a shadow of *someone* standing from a distance, standing alone, watching... The investigation ends, the teams collect their trigger objects, stationary cameras, and other equipment, and return to their vehicles. While surrounded by the safety—or so they think—of their van doors and windows, they decide to listen, if only for just a moment, to their EVP recordings: *"Help me!," "Get me away from here," "Who are you?," "Make them stop,"* and *"I'm dead?"* are all common answers revealed by the recordings. Likewise, the stationary cameras reveal that the trigger objects, just as speculated, moved void of any observable variables.

These experiences and findings are almost certain to happen to anyone who tempts the hand of the dead at Dorothea Dix. In fact, at the cemetery in Dorothea Dix Park, it is uncommon to leave without some level of paranormal findings! Not all people are ready to experience the hauntings of the old insane asylum; not all people are ready to hear a voice from beyond the grave answer his or her own questions; not all are ready to understand this matter...

Fort Macon

Carteret County

Being built in 1826, the stone work is magnificent. I am speaking of the bridge (a unique mixture of bridge and trench) which serves as the entrance to the fortified walls of Fort Macon. Yet, something seems off about this cobblestone and brick path. Perhaps the coloration? A war-beaten grayish/blackish pigment covers the cold stones. They provoke an eerie feeling of foreboding and watchfulness. Not one's own watchfulness but the feeling of *being watched.* The feeling is so strong, the strange experience could better be described as the "confirmation" of being watched. As you near the end of the

The entrance of Fort Macon.

centuries-old brick and stone, a wooden bridge lies before you. Standing where the mason ground meets the holistic wood of the bridge, the sun is blocked by the towering brick of the outer walls. The bricks are separated only by small, rectangular holes expanding the entirety of the outer wall—a place where guns and cannons can protrude while soldiers fired towards their enemies.

That was nearly 200 years ago. Now, the fort stands void of active military efforts. Glance to your right, off the bridge and over the grass is an opening in the hardened wall. If you choose to stray from the entrance, you may investigate this opening. As you get closer, you notice that, lying before you, is yet again another pathway. This time, it descends downwards to another entrance. The steps leading to the dark and damp room bear stains, cracks, and all kinds of evidence regarding their age. Attached to the brick directly above the arch-shaped entranceway is a sign. "Watch your step," it reads. Cautiously entering, you will be greeted with a rush of cool air, no matter how hot it is outside. The air is heavy with moisture and *something else*, that "feeling." It is dark; there exist only a few, small openings serving as windows or places to watch for enemies. Alas, this strange room leads to nothing, leaving you with the only choice, to wander back to the bridge and face the towering walls again. Different bricks were used to construct the impressive fort. They vary in size. Some are stones, others bricks; it appears a cement type substance may have also been used. One thing still remains, each brick, each stone, each corner of each wall and room seem to share the command to observe that unusual "dark reverence." Could it be because of the sheer size of the castle-like structure? Maybe the foreboding is brought on by knowing the number of dead bodies that littered these grounds during war times. There remains only one last choice: *enter*.

"The Bombs Bursting in Air"

Behind the large doors and walls, so tall that you now feel as if you're the size of an ant, rests a large patch of green grass. Surrounding the field are the inner walls. Composed of brick, these walls hold within them various rooms: barracks, mess halls, cells

for ammunition, ranking officer headquarters, and various other military related storage spaces. Three large stairways stand nestled around the walls, two beside each other and one across from the pair. One of the stairways bears scars similar to the stairs of which I previously spoke. Towards the middle of one of these ascending steps exists a subtle divot, a crater, on each step. The deformation was created by a cannon ball that flew over the wall and rolled down these steps during the Civil War.

Ascend the steps and you will stand looking down at the fort. Somehow, though you stand above the walls, that "feeling" remains. Stationed consistently around the upper level of the fort are large cannons, awaiting the command to fire. Glance over the walls and you will see paradise: rolling hills created to add fortification in times of battle, and the ocean. The fresh air breezes across your face as the sound of crashing waves flows through your ears. The foreboding now shares its place with a sense of tranquility. How strange it is that darkness and light seem to occupy the same space, sharing it, as if they are aware of one another. Alas, the feeling of bliss does not settle. This is the section of the fort, the very walls which you stand upon, where that "feeling" was created, those many years ago, when Benjamin Combs, Company F, of the 10th North Carolina Artillery, undertook his guard duties in 1862, during the siege of Fort Macon.

"Combs, report to guard duty," demanded the commanding officer. "Yes, sir," responded Benjamin Combs, a young, newly-married, Confederate soldier. Unknowing what was to meet him, Benjamin, in his early twenties, walked up the stairs and assumed his position as one of the guards. Sweat began to trickle towards his cheeks from beneath his gray, wool hat as his eyes slowly adjusted. "Just another day," he thought as he noted the shipless ocean. That is until he heard the first blast.

"Cannon fire!" he screamed while cupping his hands on each side of his mouth. The Union ship remained out of his vision. "BOOM!" Another blast was sent, followed by another. The fort was under attack. The heavy cannon balls, easily capable of removing a soldier's head from his shoulders smashed into the outer walls. Some cannon balls hit the upper corners of the fort's walls. Benjamin turned to find cover. As long as he was at his guard post, he was in the open and unsafe. As he neared the steps, he heard it. "SMASH!" A cannon ball touched down, exploding directly next to him, pelting the young Confederate with dirt and rocks. The dirt hit him with such force that it left lesions across his exposed skin and face. As the cannon fire exploded, it sent a large piece of the lead ball in Combs' direction, crashing into his back, thrusting him down the stairs.

Combs lay on the ground, unable to move. He screamed in agonizing pain. His ears rang from the blast. His sight remained in a state of momentary dizziness as shock set in. Field medics rushed to Benjamin. The blast broke his ribs, piercing his lungs with five of the shattered bones. Surprisingly, he was still alive. The medics gave Benjamin the best treatment they could. After hours of sickening pain, Benjamin Combs died.

The Union successfully advanced to the fort and captured it, claiming Fort Macon for the Federal Army. The siege lasted from March 23 to April 26, nearly an entire month of bloodshed.

The cannons near where Benjamin Combs was stationed.

Countless men, both Confederate, like Benjamin Combs, and Union perished during this battle. Many were not returned to their homes and families again. Countless bodies were put in the ocean waters, just a few minutes' walk outside the fort. Some of the deaths were sudden; others were prolonged and filled with the pain only found in nightmares (like Benjamin's). The ending of these soldiers' lives was so sudden and or unexpected, it should come as no surprise that many continue fighting—even today—not knowing the battle has long been over.

It's Not Over Yet

Since the siege of Fort Macon, the military structure has experienced a large amount of unexplained activity. Consider the words from a veteran park ranger who was brave enough to share his personal encounters: "Lots of people come here saying that they've seen something, heard something, or felt something. Call it what you will, but I have always leaned towards the skeptic side of things." The park ranger nervously laughed after presenting me with this bit of

A view of Fort Macon's ground level.

information. "That doesn't mean I haven't experienced paranormal things here, however," he continued while regaining composure. His personality quickly shifted to that of seriousness. He continued:

"In the mornings, when I am the only one here, I'll walk throughout Fort Macon to make sure each room is clean, nothing is out of place, and everything is set for visitors." (The fort has museum-inspired exhibit spaces in some of the rooms located within its walls.) "I was in one of the educational rooms, the Civil War room. Each room is furnished with photographs, clothing, artifacts, and educational videos and sounds associated with the topic. In this specific case, the room was decorated with Civil War guns, cannon balls, swords, clothes, and a video which demonstrates how a cannon is fired. I opened the door and entered the dim space. Shutting the door, I felt for the light switch. After turning the lights on, I walked around, looking at everything and making sure all was set."

As expected, silence filled the room only to be broken by the rhythmic, deep knocking sound caused by the park ranger's heavy work boots' impact with the wooden floor. That is, until he heard the command, "Fire!" The command was followed by the loud "booming" of a large cannon. He turned around with speed to find the educational video on cannons playing. "The only way to activate the video is by pushing a button. There is no other power buttons," explains the ranger. That famed "feeling" which fills every inch of space within the fortress walls began to overwhelm him. The rhythmic "thuds" increased to a light jog as the park ranger exited the Civil War room. "I am not sure what it was, but something was definitely there with me; I could *feel* it." A reminder by Benjamin Combs regarding his untimely death perhaps?

"That isn't the only thing to happen to us park rangers," explained the state employee. "There was another man who saw something very, shall we say, 'eerie.' At night, when we close Fort Macon, we [park rangers] might be closing by ourselves. Such was the case with this other ranger. His night began in one room within the fort. Since it was dark, the lights were on in this single room. When it was time for the ranger to close the park, he started with the room he occupied." Turning off the lights, the man paused for a moment to allow his eyes to adjust to the night. After his eyes had adjusted, he left the room, closed the door, and locked it.

"After being positive that all lights were off and all electronics were stopped for the night, the employee closed the large doors to the fort's entrance before exiting for the night." After being positive everything was safe for the night, the park ranger made his way across the wooden bridge, over the trench-like pathway, and to the main parking lot. The car park wherein his truck was is on elevated ground. Therefore, sections of the fort are visible from this parking lot. Once the man reached his truck, he turned back to look at the fort beneath the night sky. He instantly noticed something strange, the office where he began his closing efforts was once again illumined. The light was on. With no way of forming an answer as to why the light in his office was back on, the ranger, being unsettled, got in his truck and began his trip home. "He found employment elsewhere after that," concluded the veteran ranger.

The spirit, or spirits, which reside in Fort Macon do not seem to attract attention only from employees. Many visitors to the fort, as well as reenactors, share experiences and leave the fort with more than merely a history lesson. Activity seems to increase directly after a Civil War reenactment. Men dressed in both Union and Confederate uniforms demonstrate, step-by-step, how the armies loaded and fired cannons, as well as the commands used with each step on a regular basis. This form of demonstration, though educational to us, may very well be seen as triggering for any residual haunts left over from Fort Macon's Civil War days. Following the performances, visitors and volunteers claim to hear commands whispered into their ears, the faint touch of a cold hand, or the sound of cannon fire, though no one has yet to fire another cannon. It is believed that multiple souls still attempt to defend the fort. Due to one psychic intervention, we know the name of at least one of them.

When a renowned psychic visited Fort Macon, she instantly honed in on the various emotions connected to the place. After roaming from room to room, as if guided by an unseen entity, she

Fort Macon's barracks. One of the prime locations for lingering spirits.

began to speak, "There's a young man here. He was hit in the back by something. He died here in the fort."

"Are you able to find out his name?" One voice spoke up from the group of bystanders. After pausing for a moment in deep concentration, she responded, "Ben, Ben, Ben, Ben." Indeed, Fort Macon is a stunning piece of American history (as dark as the Civil War was) and exists as a never ending well of knowledge. Though I must warn the reader, be prepared to hear the hushed whispers of soldiers directly behind you and see the shadows of Civil War soldiers walking to and from their posts (perhaps even running), and above all, be prepared for battle. Some unlucky visitors experience being pushed, grabbed, or even scratched while in these walls which demand an ever-increasing level of dark reverence.

The Cotton Exchange

Wilmington, New Hanover County

Downtown Wilmington can be defined by many things. One word to describe all the outstanding restaurants, shops, historic sites, river view, and more can be as simple as "stunning." The waterfront possesses the hearts of millions (both vacationers and locals alike). Walk down the large, wooden pathway (large enough yet for foot traffic to flow on each side but with the amount of sightseers on the boardwalk, it never seems wide enough) anchored next to the Cape Fear River. Some wooden planks are older, some newer (some might even appear to be hanging on by a thread!). The

One of the signs of the Cotton Exchange.

breathtaking view of the large river causes you to look over the minor critiques of the boardwalk.

Resting within the river, so close to the path on which you are strolling, are various kinds of sea vessels. Some smaller, personal boats, such as sailboats; others, larger yachts belonging to local millionaires. Some have been converted to restaurants on the water. But none are more visible than the Battleship USS *North Carolina*, which rests a distance down the river.

The large bridge suspended across the Cape Fear River remains visible from any part of the waterfront. Yet, it somehow adds to the charm of the location as does the soft, relaxing swooshes of river water gently caressing the wood of the docks. The magical sounds of children laughing and playing, as well as your occasional heavy-paced footsteps of an afternoon or early morning jogger. The wood beneath your feet vibrates as the runner offers a friendly "Hi." or "On your left!" while passing by. Yes, stunning indeed.

The excitement of downtown Wilmington is not contained only in the waterfront. It pours out to the streets surrounding the waterfront as well. Alas, the excitement, quaintness, and charming personalities which make Wilmington a tourist destination was not always part of the city's presence. The town is home to a very unique history, a very *dark* history. During the early 18th century, the waterfront saw regular visits by pirates, murderers, and all sorts of dishonorable people. These shameful persons congregated around the taverns, eateries, and brothels which once existed on Nutt Street.

One block from Nutt Street was (and still is) Front Street. The reputable businesses made their homes on Front Street, leaving the businesses of ill repute to waste away in the decay they so frequently created. Crimes were committed in such high volume that it was not entirely uncommon to stumble upon a lifeless corpse blocking a Nutt Street drainage path. A book could be written (and probably already has been) regarding all the devilish ways which occupied the once corrupt riverside of Wilmington. With such darkness shrouding Wilmington's past, families seeking a weekend getaway are not the only tourists Wilmington attracts. Some visitors arrive at the coastal town seeking something which cannot often be seen; something to remind us of Wilmington's past...

One building sat in the what was then misfortunate position of sharing both Front and Nutt streets. Originally built in the 1800s, the location was first intended for James Sprunt's Cotton Exchange. Labeled as the East Coast's largest exporter of cotton, the Exchange was composed of eight buildings. By studying maps of the original area, the Cotton Exchange stood at 308 to 316 Nutt Street. This portion of land has since been renamed North Front Street. It stands as one of the first historical buildings in North Carolina to be refurbished. Today, the location is known as "The Cotton Exchange" and is home to countless businesses, shops, and restaurants. The Cotton Exchange has stood witnessing many crimes and disturbing happenings which occurred in the streets below (perhaps even within its walls) and has remained silent with the memories of such foul actions internalized within each brick. The newly renovated Cotton Exchange has been home to countless shops. As years come to pass, various shops close their doors and new ones Take Up the vacant spaces. Two businesses however, an art gallery and a restaurant, have managed to remain as permanent members of the Cotton Exchange family. Being part of the family, some of the long forgotten, dark history—no, dark *secrets*—hidden within the walls of the historic site has been made known to these two businesses. The owners of these two veteran locations within the Cotton Exchange have agreed to exclusive interviews. Read the following cautiously.

The Golden Gallery

Though it has moved throughout the building, the Golden Gallery has had one of the longest reigns in the Cotton Exchange. With arousing art pieces and serving various needs expressed by fellow artists and hobbyists alike, it is not difficult to see why the gallery has seen such success. The gallery is operated by the Golden family. With the gallery's life, spanning more than 45 years, one of the owner's has gotten to know every aspect of the business from creating fine art to engaging in conversations surrounding the needs of artists, and perhaps even learning one or two of the building's *secrets*...

141

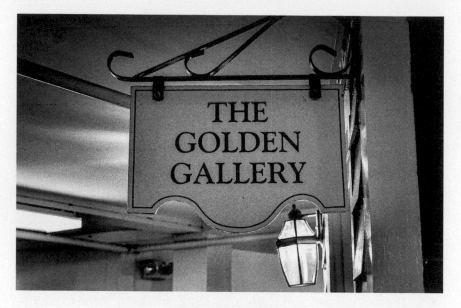

The Golden Gallery.

"I grew-up at Golden Gallery," states John Golden, one of the artists and operators of the gallery. "As a child, I remember playing with toys behind the counter, walking around the store and, when being told I was too loud, wandering the halls of the Exchange. Throughout that time, I neither saw nor heard anything paranormal." John's childhood exchanged places with teenage years only to be replaced again with adulthood. Throughout his formative years, John experienced not a single, paranormal thing happening. This would change when he introduced his wife and children to the Gallery.

"Around 2006, we stored a few of my daughter's toys in my office. She was a toddler at the time and, well, needed something to entertain her as we brought her to the Gallery while working." Perhaps it is also important to note that during these early years of Mr. Golden's fatherhood he often stayed at the Gallery late into the night. "In those days, it was up to me to ensure packages were packed, invoices were sent, and shipping materials were in place so we could get orders to customers in a timely fashion. During these late-night shifts, I'd spend my time locked away in my office, turning my attention from the never-ending stack of paperwork to a computer screen." John forced his bloodshot eyes to focus (as much as they would) on the small print on the paper. His eyes burned from exhaustion with every blink. As he glanced at the computer screen, his eyes naturally closed as his pupils rushed to adjust to the new intake of light.

He sat at his desk, examining and entering data on the documents and computer. The only audible noise which broke the endless silence was that of his fingertips clicking away at the computer's keyboard or the occasional taking up and writing with his pen. A tired, low-pitched creaking filled the otherwise empty room with each turn of his chair and accompanying each of his failed attempts to settle his back sitting in the chair. Such was the level of excitement on an average night of John's during the early 2000s. However, every once in a while, *something else* would join the classic sounds of office work.

"While I worked facing my desk, I heard a child's toy activate. A noise began to emulate from the plastic design. The quietness of the room somehow amplified the child-like song that played." John's eyebrows shifted closer as his face took on a look of confusion. "I turned around and looked towards the dark corner of my office to find one of my daughter's toys sounding off. The strangest part about this is that to activate the sounds, a small, red ball needed to be pushed through a hole located on the top of the toy. There was no other way to make the toy sound off."

At first, John concluded that the batteries must need changing. The frequency—or lack thereof—seemed to diminish this conclusion from John's mind. When toys, especially toys from the time period when this occurrence took place, needed a battery change, they began notifying the owner by sounding off. However, the activations would become more frequent and with each noise forced out from the dying toy, the music or voice would morph into a scratchy static or a demented slur of what seemed to be phrases. This was not the case in John's account. Far from it.

"It was yet another 'late night shift.' I found myself glued to the screen of my computer only to pull away to glance at an invoice, only to return to my state of screen fixation." All was still, except for the occasional chair creak, pen stroke, or key click. That is, until an alarming, unexpected noise blasted onto the scene. This time, it caused John to jump. His phone rang. "Wondering who was calling me this late at night, I paused for a moment to glance at the caller identification. It was my brother-in-law." "I need a break," thought John as he answered the incoming call.

"Hello?" "Hey, John, how are you? You working?" "I'm fine, how are you? ... Yep, but it's O.K. I'm nearly finished."

The conversation carried on for a few more minutes as John reclined in his chair. "The room wasn't quiet anymore; I was talking on the phone and was focused on the conversation. In fact, for a brief moment, I forgot I was even at work." That is, until something pulled him back into reality. "I held my phone to my left ear as I spoke with my brother-in-law. As he spoke, I remained attentive, until I heard someone speaking directly into my right ear. A little girl whispered a few sentences in my ear, opposite the one to which I was holding my phone, in the same manner as if a child tells someone her secret." John froze as his mind raced to think of any possible way that he might not be alone. To his terror, there remained no explanation.

"Hey, I've got to go. I'll call you back." John told his brother-in-law

A bird's eye view of the Golden Gallery.

in a slow, drawn-out fashion. "Oh, ok. Is anything the matter?" John's brother-in-law asked. "No, I'll call you back."

John hung up his phone and placed it back on the table. He slowly rose from his chair; creaks filled the air. ("I don't want them to know I'm on to them," thought John naturally, though he was alone.) He studied his office, nothing. He cautiously cracked his office door and peered at the empty, dark gallery; it was stiller than stone. The experience caused John to feel cold as his blood retracted from his hands and legs. He turned back to his desk, shut his workspace down for the day, and left the Cotton Exchange for the night. Though he still remembers the voice, so close to his ear, as if the girl's cold lips were touching it as she spoke, he could not make out the chilling words expressed by the entity.

Wanna Play?

The Golden Gallery has had the pleasure of existing in five separate locations throughout the historic site. Not only did these opportunities give John and his Gallery a chance to try out new projects and get to know some of the businesses that have come to pass, but it also presented a new chance to acquire yet another one of the building's *secrets*.

"Located on the Front Street level of the Cotton Exchange is a small, shoe-box location which was once home to an ice cream shop. One of our previous locations was near the shop so we got to know the owners. One day, they expressed to me a rather unsettling issue … if you want to call it an 'issue.'"

"Hi, John!" greeted the owner of the ice cream establishment.

"Hey there, how are you?" John answered.

"A bit worried, if I'm honest."

"Oh? Why's that?"

"Well…" The founder of the treat shop paused and looked around to ensure no one else was present, then continued, "Have you seen a little girl roaming around here?"

"A little girl?" John answered with concern (this was before he "met" the famed little girl).

"Yes," nervously answered the store owner. "There is a little girl who roams these halls and seems to play on the seats in front of the other shops. Sometimes I can hear her; other times, she's silent. Almost as if my hearing is momentarily lost."

"That's interesting. No, I haven't seen her. What is your concern?"

"Well, I don't think she's ... *really here.* I mean, not like you and I."

John paused, trying to articulate a response. The ice cream shop owner finally filled the awkward silence: "I think she's a ghost. From time to time she appears as if a regular, normal little girl. Other times, I see her for a split second. I watch her as she enters the ice cream shop then she vanishes, right before my eyes. When I look at the surveillance camera, she doesn't show up." John, being a gentleman, did not want to disrespect the fellow merchant. But John was aware of the local ghostly sightings many have claimed to experience within the Cotton Exchange.

"That's scary. I'm not sure what to do," John answered. The worry-stricken owner of the ice cream establishment kindly thanked John for talking and walked away. A few days passed before John heard the news. A paranormal investigation crew had been summoned to investigate the Front Street Level. As eager as John was, he was not prepared to hear what was captured ... the investigation mimicked the style of many other paranormal investigations. The team wandered the dark halls at night, projecting questions into the dark expanse, photographed areas and conducted EVP sessions. Though the investigation was similar to that of millions of others hoping to capture a ghost's presence, one thing differed: the findings:

The team heard of the complaints made by the ice cream shop. They were given permission to investigate inside the store front. Within the creamery, they targeted a specific spirit, that of a little girl. Upon reviewing the EVP session which took place within the ice cream shop, an unmistakable child's voice can be heard, "I want my ice cream."

John's Residual Haunts

Though time has passed since John first heard of the little girl— and first *heard* the little girl—the Golden Gallery stands as not only a destination for the artistic-minded individual but also the energy of souls. To this day, John regularly captures orbs on his surveillance cameras. "Roughly every ten days, I'll see orbs appear on the cameras. They vary in size and alter their shape while floating about. They even change direction as if looking for something. I've seen bugs on surveillance footage and that's [the orbs] not bugs...."

A large, framed piece of art once hung on one of John's display walls, anchored for extra protection. As he opened up shop one morning, he was greeted by the large, fine art piece lying on the floor a distance away from its original hanging position. After watching, from the surveillance cameras, the frame itself seamlessly leap from the wall and crash to the floor with such force that the glass shattered, John knew there was no other explanation other than that *someone* was beckoning his attention. More recently, while Mr. Golden works on his computer, the technology freezes and, no matter what John does, the computer refuses to function unless John asks, "Can you please stop? I really need to get this work done." At the request, the computer will return to normal functioning.

This happens at such a frequent rate, and the haunts at the Cotton Exchange have gained such notoriety, that when celebrity ghost hunters were in town, they agreed to check Mr. Golden's computer and surrounding area for any electro-magnetic interference. To everyone's surprise, the room and area was free of any observable causes for the computer errors. Ah, but our journey does not end with John Golden! I did mention The Cotton Exchange is home to two long lasting establishments...

The German Cafe

Located on the Nutt Street level of the Exchange stands the famed "German Cafe," known for its authentic German cuisine, as well as the cultured aesthetics which welcome every guest as they enter the Germanic inspired eatery. Serving guests a slice of Deutschland for nearly half a century, the restaurant is a staple for anyone wishing to indulge in fine European flavors. But what is it—aside from the impeccable dishes and traditional décor—that

The German Cafe.

beckons visitors? There exists a second reason, a lesser-known reason (*a more macabre reason*) as to why the German Cafe is visited. Some people visit the cafe in hopes of seeing *her*. She reveals her identity to those chosen only by her own discretion. One such person (the first person) she chose to reveal her presence to is Mr. Harvey Hudson, the owner and operator of the German Cafe.

"I am not very superstitious," states Harvey as he begins his mental revisiting of the daunting experience. "That being said, there is one experience I will never forget nor am I capable of dismissing. For the first time in a long time, I had a real sense of fear when I realized I wasn't alone. I didn't let anyone in and the doors were all locked. I was in there [the German Cafe] with that *thing*."

Many years ago (though remembered as if it had just occurred), it was time for the restaurant to close for the night. Harvey stood in the middle of the first floor of his establishment and panned the room. "Everyone's out," he thought as he began walking to the polished, wooden stairs; he decided to enter the second level of the cafe to make sure everyone was out. "Empty," he thought as he stood on the second floor in a similar fashion as he observed the empty chairs and tables stationed on the first floor. After being satisfied with his observations, Harvey repeated the task on the third floor. His instinctual sense was correct; he was alone in the darkened restaurant.

He inspected each, spotless creaking step as he made his way down the stairway. Once again on the first level, he made his way towards the kitchen while all along inspecting the freshly swept floor. Before entering the kitchen, the man gazed at his resting restaurant. A sense of pride and satisfaction welled up within him as he sighed a breath of relief before beginning his final task for the night: turning the lights off. Various lights on each level shut off, one by one, as he switched the desired switches. The establishment was quiet, almost as if it were sleeping for the night. A hushed sense began to well up within him once more. This time, it was of eerie origins. The longer he stared at the now barely lit levels, the stronger his sense of foreboding grew. The "feeling" arrived to such a state that it might disturb the cafe's slumber.

The doorway wherein Harvey found himself presents a clear view to both the second and third levels. All the while, the sense of darkness magnified, "I haven't felt that feeling in a very long time," retells Harvey. "As the feeling intensified, I began to check my surroundings. I looked up from the doorway to the third level." His eyes instantly fixated on the third level balcony; or rather, the two, lifeless hands which grasped the aged wood. "I saw an elderly lady standing over the balcony. She wore a Confederate gray, antebellum dress. Her older age was made clear by the spectacles which resided on the bridge of her nose and her gray hair pulled back into a bun." There she stood, stiller than still, before Harvey. Her gaze pierced through the fear-filled man as he froze, unable to deflect his fixed vision.

"Her expression was ... unique. At first, I was mortified. I instantly knew what I was seeing. As I registered her perplexed expression, I felt as if she was sending a message." After coming to grips with what he was seeing (or at least as much as he could in that situation) Harvey believes that the ghostly apparition was not

The balcony on which "the Ghost" is seen.

standing there to strike him with fear. He felt rather that she was sending a message, "I'm here. Don't worry." Harvey's logic kicked in once again as he blinked and quickly shook his head when attempting a double-take. "When I looked back in the woman's direction, she had turned towards the doorway next to her, and walked away."

Perhaps the most flabbergasted he had ever been, Harvey paused his exiting as he stood in the same doorway from which he spotted the lifeless corpse and replayed the scenario, etching the woman's image deep into his long-term memory. Throughout the years, Harvey has never forgotten the sighting of the portly, short woman. A strange mix of disturbance and comfort well within him as he remembers her exaggerated presence.

"I have not seen her since that one experience. But, whenever I am alone in the German Cafe, I can feel her presence," remarks Harvey. Mr. Hudson, as well as others who have been lucky enough to encounter the Ghost, as she is often named, feel honored, but morbidly terrified...

Over the years, countless customers and employees have experienced strange and unexplainable happenings in the German Cafe. Some hear voices (perhaps the Ghost's voice?); others see flashes of light and orbs; objects moving and physical contact are even reserved for select groups. However, the mysterious ghost woman very rarely shows herself. Photographers claim to have captured shadows and other strange phenomena on film but never the Ghost. It is known that a violent fire engulfed that very section of the Cotton Exchange in its early years. Some victims managed to escape while others remained trapped until their flaming ends. Could this woman have been some kind of an overseer, perhaps? Maybe she was one of the victims. A definite answer is far from possible when attempting to identify the Ghost. There is an ever-increasing number of customers coming to the German Cafe for authentic German food but leaving with a grisly reminder of the souls which still linger (even to this day!). Only one statement can be agreed upon: The German Cafe is authentically haunted.

The German Cafe's entrance way.

Haunts in Every Corner

Do not think that avoiding the Golden Gallery and the German Cafe will cause you to escape whatever nightmarish reality awaits you at the Cotton Exchange. Do not be mistaken! Haunts of every kind reside in every level, every walkway, every nook and cranny of the Exchange. Towards Front Street, charming haunts (if there exists such a thing as a "charming haunt") occur such as the sight of two small children, a boy and a girl, playing on the benches and running past unexpected visitors. Sometimes, their laughter and footsteps can be heard; other times it is silent. In the same level, a soldier, adorned in what many claim to be a Revolutionary War uniform, is spotted leaning against the centuries-old brick. Towards on the Nutt Street level, rambunctious vocal cues as well as the musical notes of an old rag-time or "honky-tonk" piano can be heard during the night. Even though it is hundreds of years too late, the blood-curdling screams of victims begging for help are regular occurrences. There is as well as the small yell of a young boy calling for his mother. Yes, every room, every path, and every brick which comprises the Cotton Exchange is waiting to share their dark and mysterious secrets with anyone.

Dead Men Tell No Tales

Wilmington,
New Hanover County

Welcome aboard the USS *North Carolina*, a most *mysterious* battleship. The *North Carolina* served during the "Great War," or as it is most commonly called "World War II." She stands as the most decorated American vessel of the Second World War. This battleship served from 1941 to 1947. Today, she is docked, commemorating those over 10,000-plus North Carolinians who lost their lives during World War II. The USS *North Carolina* carried 2,400 sailors; only 18 of them

The USS *North Carolina*.

died aboard. This is a tour, but not one's normal exploration of the history of a battleship. History is the subject of things lost to time. What we will now explore is very much present. Oh yes, I should know, along with me *it* is watching you board *its* ship...

The Office of the Executive Officer

Due to the nature of this journey, we will begin at the ship's administration office. Here in this small space is where sailors as well as officers manned their posts. This was a post where individuals entered by invitation only. It was not a welcoming area for those without an invitation. As you can imagine, this office held main communication lines, information from higher officials, tasks, and sensitive information belonging to the ship's officers. Needless to say, it should come as no surprise as to why this area demanded such high-level security. Eighty years after the War, it seems that the discipline drilled into those charged with duties in this communications office lasts a lifetime ... perhaps even longer.

The unwelcoming manner is felt today. A man is often spotted in this office. Yet this *man* is unlike you and me. At times he is a uniformed sailor; other times he is nothing more than a spectral figure, a frightening shadow, at times, a misty fog. This apparition is seen, almost on cue, walking near the gun turret just over there, by the office entrance, and entering the office. At night, employees watch a man walk into this space. Those who chose to follow this gentleman report, having peered into the office, that the room is filled with nothing but nautical objects. This unknown soldier is observed so frequently it is not uncommon for employees and volunteers who see him to exclaim, "Hello, shipmate, how are you?" This *shipmate* remains silent.

Some visitors ask their guides who the man is standing in the office but, the guides are unable to respond for the office is always empty. Perhaps he is unaware of the presence of the living. Perhaps he is even unaware of the remarkable passing of time wherein he was once part of the living for which he now has no recollection. Perhaps our friend, shipmate, is unaware that his own mortality has expired.

From time to time, this faithful sailor reveals his purpose when confronted. It is tradition for paranormal investigators to conduct work on the USS *North Carolina*. Some are hobbyists, others are celebrities. Regardless of status, the sailor at present stands firm by his orders pertaining to the communication area. As a group of ghost hunters investigated this very office, they chose to conduct an EVP (Electronic Voice Phenomena) session in hopes of hearing the voice of a man who breathed his last. They tried connecting with the spirit by asking various questions, "Hello, sailor. Where are you from?" "How long have you been *in* [enlisted]?" "Is this your first tour?"

After each question, the team sat in silence, hoping that the recorder would capture a voice inaudible to the naked, human ear. After the allotted time ceased, the investigators stopped the recording, played back the questions, and listened with undivided attention. Each question was answered by silence or perhaps the faint sound of a loud vehicle passing over the bridge adjacent to the ship. They decided to hold another EVP session—this time with more pointed questioning.

"Why are you hiding?" The moment this question left the hunter's mouth, chills engulfed the seasoned investigators. The room dropped noticeably in temperature, and the paranormal team felt instant regret. Despite this, the team continued their routine: sit, wait, then listen back. After again waiting, the time deemed sufficient for a haunting answer to be provided, recording was paused again. Hearts jumped and slight body quivers were felt as they listened to the EVP playback, "Why are you hiding?"

"Get out." The team clearly and undoubtedly heard the soldier's order. The investigators were occupying space, with permission yet, without invitation...

Stay.... Forever!

Let us draw your attention to the Combat Information Center or C.I.C. as it is known among the crew. The information contained within the C.I.C. was highly classified. If so much as the smallest detail of data were revealed to even a single person, the outcome for

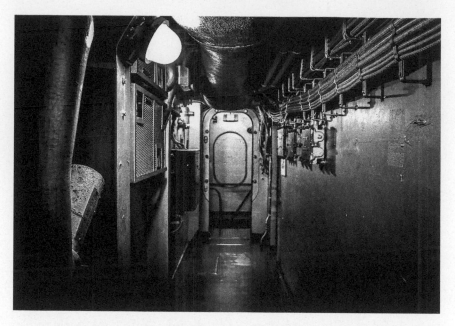

One of the many corridors aboard battleship *North Carolina*.

Battleship *North Carolina* could have been catastrophic; at least, *more* catastrophic than it already was...

All sailors knew the importance of the Combat Information Center and ensured that only individuals on a "need-to-know-basis," such as high-ranking officers, were able to attend briefings. This standard, which was observed by all aboard the *North Carolina*, kept men stationed in close proximity to the C.I.C. when meetings or important information was within her secretive walls. These men committed hours of their lives guarding the large, hinged door which served as the entrance, the only entrance, to the C.I.C. It is my understanding that some of these men were not only willing to commit hours to their guarding posts, but eternities.

While exploring the *North Carolina*, and seeking ways to better interpret the historical significance of each section of the ship, two employees roamed from room to room; space to space; and deck to deck. This thought-provoking walk guided the employees to the entrance of the now empty Combat Information Center. Without hesitation, the staff entered the once forbidden area. Occupied with the current task, the employees continued their conversation as they walked deeper into the Center.

"How can we bring to life what took place in this room?" one employee asked the other. Before the latter could answer, a slight, high-pitched creaking was heard, both people turned toward the direction of the spine-shivering noise only to watch the main door, on the other side of the room, close. "SLAM!" The employees found the door closing rather strange; this is a solid, heavy door which no level of wind can sway.

The employees paused their conversation as they retraced their steps to the now closed entrance. One of the staff members grabbed the circular door handle and pulled the door with enough force to open it. The door did not open. The other employee attempted to regain their only way out. This attempt ended in failure as well. The door was not only closed, but locked. At this point, the employees saw the mixture of fear, stress, and anxiety which both individuals tried to contain but showed ever so clearly on their faces. "Keep calm," they thought. This is a professional setting after all. The first employee then rotated the heavy handle and was able to open the door. They both left with haste. The remainder of their historical conversation was filled with many pauses and the ability to hold attention was lost as the two spent the rest of their time on the *North Carolina* pondering the freakish happening.

Something very clearly forced the door shut and successfully locked it, cutting off the poor staff members' only way out. Why might someone—or *something*—do this? Perhaps as one seeks to discover concealed information, one might be unable to find it. Perhaps, the entity in charge of guarding the Combat Information Center realized that, if the spirit reveals today—even that small amount—of truth regarding the happenings upon USS *North Carolina*, the facts will be too much for us, the living, to handle.

The Ward

Welcome to the next portion of our rather unusual tour. Unlike the common tour you might experience while visiting battleship

North Carolina, we are going to focus on this area: the wardroom pantry. The wardroom contains stories of everyday life aboard the battleship; nothing of interest to *us*. The pantry for the wardroom however, seems to contain some stories left to be untold by the ordinary tour guides. Why are they not mentioned, you might ask?

Adjacent to the main wardroom, we find ourselves standing in this smaller section known as the wardroom pantry. Notice the stainless-steel tables which surround us. The pantry once held vital objects and utilities used by the everyday sailor aboard this ship but, again, that much does not matter to us. Allow me to explain: two faithful members of the cleaning staff willingly undertook the elbow-aching task of polishing the tables. Due to the number of tables, one man began to work on one of the tables just there, around that corner, while the other gentleman focused upon a table here in the corner. The two members of the cleaning crew were, at this point, unable to see each other unless they left their tables and walked around the corner to the other employee. They were both alone, in their separate areas, cleaning, buffing, and polishing.

After cleaning any stains, dust, and small objects from the tables' surfaces, the men repeated the same steps. They sprayed the tables with their liquid-polishing combination, patiently waited five minutes, and wiped the polish from the table with the designated rag, then polished it with a dry rag. The duo continued these steps until they felt as if the shine emanating from the cool smooth table-tops was perfect. While the man in charge of cleaning this corner table was waiting while the liquid sat, goosebumps appeared running down his arms. The temperature had unexpectedly plummeted. Almost simultaneously, he felt a forceful hand tightly grasp the back of his leg. The man noted the force which followed. The initial impact was executed with such force, it was at first confused with his team member slapping the back of his leg. Seconds later, the uncomfortable man felt the hand not retract from slapping him but tighten. He felt the imprint of the hand's five fingers tightly around the muscle of his calf.

The now frightened man quickly turned around expecting to find his cleaning partner laughing behind him. Instead, he was faced with the wall on the opposite side of the empty area. He paused his polishing to confront his co-worker about the puzzling stimulus, "Hey, I have to ask you something..." The man began sporting a face of otherworldly bewilderment, "Did you..."—"Feel someone walk up behind me and tightly grab my leg? Yes."

Based on the man's face, the second employee was able to finish the first one's sentence. The confused (and now terrified) man had no words with which to respond. He simply finished this one table and left the ship. You see, dear guest, the cleaning man around the corner had been employed longer than the one charged with polishing this corner table. He knew of the ghosts which haunt the ship therefore, after seeing his co-worker's face, he knew that he too experienced the strange phenomenon. Though he worked on the *North Carolina* longer, he had yet to be grabbed by an unseen entity with such violence. The two men never did return to being the only two on the ship.

The Sickbay

Welcome to the sickbay. This is the portion of the ship where most people express feelings of discomfort. Some of the negative feelings stem from learning about the gruesome actions which took place here. The remaining portions of the foreboding feelings derive from *something else;* we'll get to that in a moment. Firstly, I would like for you to discover the unimaginable horrors which took place in this very section. Yes, it is true that sick sailors were sent here for treatment. However, many causes for being sent to this sickbay were due to injuries. The ship's surgeons, doctors, and assistants often raced against time to save the lives of soldiers who were stricken with life-threatening injuries. Some of these injuries were due to battle, such as those unfortunate souls sent here from the torpedo blast which attacked USS *North Carolina*; other men were sent here after accidental mishaps which ultimately ended in the losing of their lives. This is the ship's triage center, with the elongated, metallic operating table. These sailors were thrown upon this very surface in hopes that the doctor might somehow save their battered bodies.

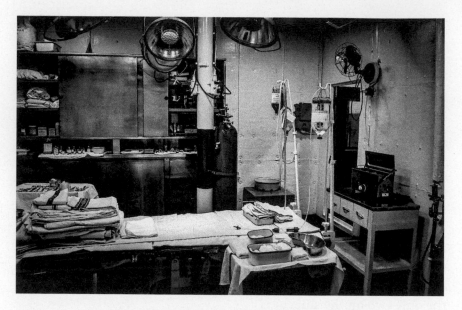

Operating Room aboard battleship *North Carolina*.

Most of the men who laid upon this table did not leave it with their lives intact.

Most people who enter this space note some level of unexplainable phenomena. The sounds of bed springs creaking, as if someone is tossing and turning, unable to sleep. The sound of people talking on in hushed tones; even the sound of agonizing screams can be heard from inside the surgical room. This area serves as a keen point of interest to many paranormal investigators. It is battleship *North Carolina*'s custom to allow an employee to accompany any paranormal investigators while performing an investigation. In this instance, two employees partook in the investigation.

The ship was silent as the investigation continued into the early morning hours. The team, along with the two employees, entered the sickbay. They chose to conduct an EVP session while in the triage room, the portion of the sickbay which experienced the highest level of emotion, trauma, and death. The team seated themselves against the back wall while the two employees reclined adjacent to the team in this corner. They opened the session with pointed questions, "Were you sick?" "Were you here because of the torpedo blast?" "Did you die on this table?" As is normal protocol for such sessions, the ghost hunters paused between each question to give time to record any potential answers. After they concluded their Q&A with the spirits, they listened to the recording in hopes of discovering new findings. As the investigators concentrated on the sounds emanating from their hand-held recording device, the employees took the opportunity to stretch their legs out and rest their weary heads upon the cold wall. This small time of tranquility was quickly shoved away by uncontrollable fear. After a few seconds passed they opened their eyes ever so slightly to ensure they would not doze off. Through the crack of their eyelids, they saw a light emanating from nothingness directly before them.

This light caused them both to jolt into upright position as their eyes became fixed on the ghostly orb. The supernatural energy appeared before them, suspended; they both observed the strange purplish/bluish coloration (similar to that of a bruise) of the light. After approximately eight seconds, the orb gently dissipated. The two employees could not mutter so much as a single syllable for the remainder of the investigation and remained in a constant state of heart-stopping fear until the morning sun was again in view.

A common experience shared by men who enter this surgical room is the unexpected shockwave of adrenaline which is activated by a strong attack. On a regular basis, men report some type of unseen force deliberately hitting their chest. This impact to the chest is sometimes followed by a strange burning sensation. The most frightening of attacks occurred during yet another paranormal investigation. As a team member thought of ways to provoke any present undead energies that might be around him to communicate, he decided to lie on the operating table. The man cautiously placed his legs towards the bottom. Once his body was completely on the cold steel, and his posture in a sitting position, he held his nerves as he gently reclined until the back of his head met the freezing temperature of the table, sending a wave of chills down his body.

The team member began to speak, bringing attention to the fact that he now lay in the same spot so many knew as their death-bed. He continued his vocal taunts until a heavy fist slammed down just below his sternum. The air left the investigator's lungs as his brain scrambled to detect the location of the threat. This was unsuccessful as the threat remained unseen. Within a blink of an eye, the team member leaped from the sickbay table. As his feet met the solid floor, he felt relief for but a moment until the pain forced him over in a hunched position. His hands placed on the edge of the table supported his collapsing body as he experienced an intensifying sensation of burning within his chest. Riddled and horrified, the man struggled to flee the room. As soon as he managed to leave, the sensation ceased and the man regained all levels of normality.

Permit me, if you would be so kind, to share with you my personal favorite from this eerie place. Yes, the painful shrieks, creaking of the bed springs, physical attacks, and even full body apparitions are all part of the USS *North Carolina* sickbay's daily life. This is

The surgical table aboard battleship *North Carolina*.

rather impressive, in a twisted fashion, but it is not *all* attributed to this space. An increasingly common report, experienced by all people, whether it be male or female, employee or volunteer, is that of the smells. As people enter this space, the very place where unsuccessful operations were carried out, there are odors of medical alcohol and burning. Perhaps the alcohol accompanies the apparition of the ship's surgeon or assistance. What of the burning smell, however? Records exist of a certain victim, a burn victim who was transferred from the carrier, the *Ticonderoga*, where he accumulated the burns, to the USS *North Carolina* for treatment. The man was found dead in his bed the next morning.

The Mess Deck and Hall

The mess deck. It was once filled with sailors, shoulder to shoulder, conducting various activities. Some partook in hobby activities, friendly conversations, games and music, but most of the men within this room utilized this space to enjoy a nice meal (at least as nice as one can get while aboard a battleship). There was once a time, those many years ago, when the sounds of many voices and hard soles tapping against the ship's floor filled this deck. Now it is utterly silent and filled with nothing but the cold, damp air and us, of course. But are we *really* the only ones occupying this space?

Gaze in that direction: do you spot it, the cooking equipment? Notice the pots, pans, and utensils neatly placed. These objects are often forced to the floor with such an impact that the sound of the two types of metal echo throughout this deck. Other times, pans are removed from their stations and placed in completely random locations only to be found once someone accidentally stumbles across them. Other times, these pots and pans are placed in various positions as if someone had made an attempt to prepare a meal. The most peculiar variable of all of these "cookery relocations" is that no one is ever present when an object is moved. If one is present when cookware flings from the walls or countertops to the floor, they are never close enough to have aided. People simply hear the resonating clinking of forks or the resounding bong of a pot contacting

The Mess Hall aboard battleship *North Carolina.*

the floor. Most individuals label these occurrences as coincidental. Others are lucky enough to witness the object seamlessly sail from one location to another. Unlike the first set of people who hear what they believe to be a mere coincidence, the ones who watch the mysterious phenomena realize the truth about the mess deck: they are not the only ones occupying it...

Much more occurs in this section of the ship. It appears as if the poltergeist, or poltergeists, who exist on this level enjoy making themselves known. We've been on our feet for a prolonged period of time as we observe with suspense each section of this battleship. I would offer you a seat on these many benches which line each side of these cafeteria-like tables. However, I will decline to do so in fear that you will not complete the tour. You see, as people, employee and visitor alike, rest upon these benches, countless victims report feeling the sensation of one end of the bench (the end closest to the one sitting on the bench) being lifted into the air only to be moved either forward or backward before meeting the floor once more— with force, as if someone suspending a single side of the bench with his hands has unexpectedly let go. The chilling part is that these sensations are not some sort of illusion carried out by the psyche but in fact occur in reality.

But wait! Our unseen, mischievous fellows do not stop there. On rare occasions, these sailors will surprise bystanders in incomprehensible ways. Consider an account one employee will never forget: this person stood in this very room while she discussed ideas for their upcoming "haunted ship" event. She spoke of plans regarding the area with another co-worker. This occurred after hours so the two were the only ones present on the ship ... or so they thought. This employee asked the other person a question on the topic the two presently discussed. As the co-worker responded, the employee saw the unmistakable, full-body shadow of a man walk behind the second employee. This shadow walked across the room and up the ladder. As the apparition crossed the room, there was no audible sound. This factor alone was enough to cause a flurry of unsettling emotions.

She interrupted her co-worker and provided an explanation for the command to stop talking. The second employee took no offense but began to share the employee's fear. After checking the area for anyone else and realizing that they were the only living ones aboard, the conversation was postponed until the following workday. It is said that if you wish to see this peculiar shadow man yourself, look for him by the ladder on mess decks seven and eight. He is seen running up and down the ladders as if he exists in a time outside of time, actively carrying out ship orders. The high-pitched thuds of his military issued boots are heard as he climbs each ladder.

Engine Room

I bid you a chilling welcome as you enter the engine room. Did you notice the drop in temperature as we entered the room? Do not be alarmed ... yet. This is a common phenomenon which occurs directly before a ghostly sighting takes place. Personally, I would expect nothing less. After all, this is the most paranormally active section of the ship. Odd, isn't it? Why would the engine room serve as a paranormal hot spot? The sheer number of verified encounters that have scared countless people over the years and which took place in this very space are so many that to hear them all, a specialized tour focusing on this one room would need to be implemented. This adventure is one-of-a-kind. I will relay only those which are certain to leave anyone disturbed.

I did mention that this area is a paranormal hot spot. The less impressive run-ins with entities beyond the grave include walking into this room only to see maintenance workers, decorated in 1940s-style uniforms, conducting routine work on these large engines which sit before us. Though these crewmen seem to be carrying out hard, labor-intensive tasks on the machines, there are never sounds accompanying the men's movements. When one of the men touches the thick metal casing with an equally solid tool, or when they are bending a piece of metal with a mallet to fit a desired angle, or simply tightening these large bolts, there are no noises; each task is seen (with striking clarity, I might add), yet the room is audibly empty. Alas, these apparitions, or demented time-loops, last but a small moment before they vanish altogether. But this is merely one encounter with the dead. Many more types of "unnatural run-ins" make their homes here.

One night, as the waterfront acquired a peaceful lull and the ship was unoccupied, two faithful volunteers boarded the battleship *North Carolina* in hopes of repairing the ramps that serve as the entrance and exit to this haunted room. The night seemed to carry on just as the two expected. The night air possessed a certain quietness which instantly stirs up a sense of peace. The ship appeared to be resting, as if it was sleeping after a trying day at sea and was filled with the random creaking of the metal walls. The ceiling and floors rested due to the change in temperature from the sun exchanging its role with the moon, and the knocks and bangs brought on by the volunteers' work which, at this point, echoed throughout the ship.

The two devoted participants worked the night away. As they reached the finishing portion of their work, they noticed a strong decrease in the room's temperature. This decline was so steep that it caused the men to gain a slight shiver. "Is there an A.C. vent in here?" One of the men asked the other as he wished he brought a jacket. "No," answered the other in a confused tone. "It hasn't been cold all night." "I know, I'm not sure what's going on."

The two tried shrugging the strange, winter-like air away as they gathered their equipment and cleaned the now finished job site. After the volunteers felt that they have completed the work to the desired standards, they did not stay to chat. It was late and the frigid air continued to grow colder. Grabbing the bags brought aboard with them, they shut the lights off, causing the room to match the color of the black night sky. They then began to make their way towards the exit. They walked in a single-file line when, as they reached the middle of the room, the man following heard an unmistakable voice whisper in his ear, "I'm tired." The disembodied male voice made the volunteer jump, as it, along with the now completely darkened room, stimulated the man's senses. "Did you hear that?" The man asked with a quivering voice. "Hear what? Are you all right" His partner answered.

"I just heard a voice whisper, 'I'm tired.' Right in my ear. It was right next to me." Hearing this, the leading man stopped dead in his stride as they listened to hear if anyone else was in the room. It was utterly silent. All clues provided by their surroundings indicated they were the only two in the room. Their hearts skipped a beat then began to beat uncontrollably hard. They began to sweat. The volunteers remained in this state of fear and dread as they made their way through each level of the ship, down each darkened hallway, passed each opened door to an even darker room, through each small doorway, cautiously around each corner, accompanied by nothing but the blackness of the night and the sporadic creaking of the ship.

With each creak, the men grew increasingly petrified, nearing the point of panic. At last, they found their way through the ever-thickening darkness and to the exit off the ship. These poor modern maintenance men could not so much as sleep a wink for the remainder of the night. Today, the engine room is approached with foreboding hesitation and no one enters the haunted engine room after hours ... unless they have completely lost their minds...

Machine Shop

Perhaps the restlessly residual dead sailors who refuse to give up their posts feel as if the modern maintenance and cleaning crews are attempting to assume the duties from the seamen of old. We shall see why I have arrived at this hypothesis—maybe, just maybe, any visitors would arrive at a similar conclusion as to why these stuck souls create such terror-filled work environments for today's tradesmen. Welcome to the USS *North Carolina*'s machine shop!

Ships of this stature carried a fully functioning machine shop nestled below her decks. The night cleaning crew waited until the ship's operating hours had expired and not a soul remained aboard. On this particular, fateful night, the group planned to focus on the machine shop. They retraced the same, ritualistic steps just as they have done many nights before to board the ship. They crossed the bridge which suspended them, for a moment, over the waters, stepped upon the ship's main deck, and began their descent through each level, each hatch, down each case of ladder-like stairs, until they reached the shop.

Their trained eyes instantly focused on the dust that lay upon the surface of some of the tables, the cobwebs that adorned almost every corner of the room, and the footprints left from the countless tourists which passed through this very room. It hasn't been cleaned in a while. "We have our work cut out for us tonight, boys," said the crew leader as he began his tradition of delegating tasks to his men. After his equipment and cleaning supplies were made ready to tackle the many, unclean obstacles before him, he strolled deeper into the unkempt space only to turn back to observe his team actively unloading their cleaning tools. The man walked in this direction. He approached a corner located here on the starboard side, around this corner, one can see, are racks on which sailors casually reclined when a momentary rest from their otherwise exhausting labor was in order. As the leader turned to this corner, he peered to the right, studying each rack.

The sight of the racks did not surprise him. He had ventured to this third deck many times. The sailor sitting on the rack did, however. As the night cleaning team's leader slowly turned his head to inspect the racks on the left, his eyes, now shocked and opened wide, saw a uniformed sailor sitting on the rack. His curved back as he slouched forward, appearing to have his gaze glued to the floor, as if

The crews' racks where an apparition was seen.

he was presently in deep contemplation, was the first note the cleaner recalls. The soldier sat with his legs dangled over the side of the rack. His freshly shined, black shoes stood out to the cleaner as he tried to remain as still and quiet as humanly possible.

No matter how quiet and still our cleaning friend remained, the slouched man stayed even more still, unnaturally still. There were no noises such as the rhythmic sound of air flowing through the man's nostrils only to be exhaled with an equally recognizable sound. In like manner, the sailor's back did not raise, ever so slightly, as does every living creature that breathes air. The stillness and lack of audible variables associated with life caused the bystander's mind to shut down. He was not alive but was observable. "Could this body have been a dead man propped in an upright, slouching position by some sick person?" was the pointed question generated by the viewer's mind as his brain scrambled to make sense of the nonliving site. Suddenly the unnaturally still man leaped from the rack. A medium-toned "thud" was heard as his shined shoes met the floor. He was now standing.

The bravery which once belonged to the maintenance fellow quickly diminished at the sight of the now lifeless body which slowly turned to face this late-night intruder. The sailor did not lift his head nor move an inch, yet knew of the employee's unwanted presence. When he did lift his head, the soldier's face was pale, frightfully pale. His eyes were sunken into his skull; dark, heavy bags rested directly beneath the eyes, which were void of life. The employee's heart ramped to an uncontrollably heavy pace, which caused spells of dizziness. The sailor stood before the man for a brief moment, which felt like eternity, before advancing, gracefully, with a slight pause between each step, towards the horrified crew leader. The faint man's vision successfully fooled his brain as he witnessed a dead man walking.

Though his mind was in a state of breakdown, he still noticed the sailor's light blue button-down shirt, his dark blue service pants, and the black belt which separated the two. The deceased sailor took a total of three steps, as his eyes of death pierced the man's soul, before dismissing himself. Slowly, the apparition became engulfed by nothingness and stood before the frightened man no more. The room returned to a state of normality, filled with nothing but the racks. Unable to keep up with the dramatic spikes of adrenaline and emotions, the man succumbed to his daze and collapsed to the floor with a resounding crash.

At the sound of the crew lead's large body hitting the floor, the team dropped their tasks and rushed around the corner. They found their leader on the ground, his face as pale as the ghost he had just encountered. The difference is, this man was breathing. The team captain could not speak nor could he move for the next 30 minutes. After regaining strength, he explained his run-in with death. This account left chills and goosebumps down the back and arms of each man present. They quickly packed their belongings and left the ship in a permanent state of fear. To this day, none of the men will enter the machine shop alone.

The crew finished their job during the daylight and thought that this switching of time wherein they conducted their cleaning would somehow protect them from another paranormal encounter. Truth be told, no one is safe. As soon as you agree to climb aboard this *living* ship, you enter a nightmare.

A couple of weeks had passed since our poor fellow had his lifeless encounter of heart-attack proportions. The traumatized man boarded the battleship to conduct a routine cleaning tour of the ship. He began on the main deck, the boarding deck, and worked his way down through the levels of the ship. He found himself yet again on the third deck. This time, he was alone. He refused to enter the same dreadful place of the unforgettable happening. This time, he was merely in the same vicinity. His sweat glands activated as his natural fight or flight instincts began to wake. He paused his cleaning to glance at his surroundings. Some entryways were shut, others were opened; signs hung on the walls containing historical notes of artifacts and explaining the usage of the section.

He was indeed alone. Taking a deep breath, he forced the stressful breath out of his lungs while simultaneously relaxing his shoulders, which made them droop slightly. "Get a grip," he said to himself. He closed his eyes. As his eyelids covered his pupils, he felt the breath of someone behind him. The breath smacked the center of the back of his neck. The wind was full of such force, there existed no other explanation. Someone, or *something*, just blew on the back of his neck. The frightfully icy air caused shivers to overtake his spine as they worked their way down his body. Sparing not even a second, the man turned in the direction of the exit and sprinted upwards, through each deck, until he felt the sun's warm rays touching his frozen skin.

Cleaning crews do not seem to be the only target to the machine shop's haunts; as stated, it appears to be tradesmen. A restoration team tried their hand at repairing a few pieces and adapting the machine shop to some modern changes; oh, what a mistake that was...

Often, it is the case that these craftsmen create on-the-job tools to aid in the completion of a project. Such was the case with this group of restorers. In order to complete the last task they wished to alter within the room, they created a metal hood that would act as a wedge and secure the men's safety. After the steel hood was no longer necessary, one of the restorers placed it in the tool crypt (a fitting name). The crypt is used to store various tools and fasten them so they would not be thrown about if the battleship experienced any tremendous waves.

Once the project was completed and the time came for these modern handymen to collect their personal tools and conduct a final cleaning of the shop, the team came together to clean the area. After that, the team once more ascended through the ship. When reaching the boarding deck, the man who placed the metallic hood inside the tool crypt recalled his placement of the hood and knew it was his obligation to retrieve the piece from inside the crypt. After making this mistake known to the rest of the team, he alone began his descent through the ship and into the crypt.

He entered the empty space. His eyes spotted the metal he sought as he walked towards the tool crypt. Entering the crypt, the man reached towards the steel hood he crafted. Just as the tip of his fingers came in contact with the cold, hardened metal, someone let out a heavy sigh. It sounded like it belonged to a little girl. It came from within the crypt. The uneasy sigh was then followed by laughter. The high-pitched glee confirmed his theory that it was, in fact, a little girl. The man retracted his hand as he stood upright, snapping his head from side to side in an attempt to locate the source of the laughter. At first, he was overwhelmed with confusion. The team were the only people occupying the area minutes before his return. Due to the utter silence of the space when he entered, he undoubtedly recognized he was alone.

The handy-man's state of confusion morphed into waves of fright as the small, innocent laughter transformed into the laughter of a mature woman. This phenomenon lasted but a moment before the other worldly laughter altered again into that of an elderly woman, facing the end of her life. Though the demented laughter changed, it continued to remain in this small, confined space alongside him. The man's shallow breaths echoed throughout this machine shop as the woman's voice began to travel. Slowly, the unsettling, perhaps sinister, laughter drifted out of the crypt and across the room, the laughter mimicked that of someone overcome with joy and then deep

The tool crypt aboard battleship *North Carolina*.

sorrow. At times, it sounded as if the woman was wailing only to then trick the man by uncontrollable laughter. The disturbing sounds bounced from wall to wall and machine to machine, before dissipating into thin air, leaving nothing but a few, smaller echoes until they too returned to nothingness.

The man paused with fear and listened intently. The room returned to its former state. Just as he thought, he was the only one inside the crypt; he was the only one inside this room. His quivering hands extended once more towards the hood for which he originally re-entered the shop. As quietly as he could, he picked it up and carried it, briskly departing from the ghostly atmosphere. When he surfaced from the ship once more, he was reluctant to speak of his encounter in fear that his teammates would find him no longer fit to operate potentially dangerous machinery.

Though the voice's echoes from the machine shop ceased, they did not do the same within the man's head. There they continued to bounce back and forth. That night, while the men enjoyed a dinner together to celebrate another successful job, he let his emotions, which he held bottled within for the greater portion of that day, be known. As he expounded upon the scariest thing to ever happen to him, his fellow workers watched him and listened in silence. After he finished recalling his experience, they remained silent, unable to offer any form of response. They did not find him crazy, for they saw the authentic expressions on his face which he could no longer hold back and the fear which welled up within his eyes.

Turret Number Two

There is another place of haunting proportions to share with you. On behalf of the undead souls who linger here, welcome to turret number two. By this time, one has noticed the theme of employees roaming the ship's many rooms and decks in hopes of new ways to bring to life the history of the battleship. "How can we showcase what this turret was used for?" mused the staff members as they studied the space. Facts based upon the turret's original intent flashed in their minds as they pondered.

This section of the ship was designed specifically with war in mind. The turret was the masterfully crafted section of the ship

Turret number two. One of the many paranormal hot spots aboard ship.

whereon a large, mounted gun, able to shoot down airplanes and sink enemy ships, sat. In times of battle, sailors, often two, rushed inside of the turret to join the chaotic, sea-swaying fight. One man operated the gun as the other loaded. "Ah!" exclaimed one of the staff members. "That's it! Why don't we place two, life-size cutouts in the shape of people, positioned in similar positions as those who were stationed here would have found themselves as they operated in this space?" The co-workers loved the idea. It was a way to give visual cues as to what life was like aboard the ship during war time and could transcend language barriers. Plus, it was more entertaining than a simple sign filled with words crammed together.

The team set to work. They acquired two large sheets of P.V.C. and successfully cut and shaped it into the likeness of men. After satisfaction with the pieces was enjoyed by all on that team of employees, they strategically anchored the two sailor cutouts into their new homes. A new, somewhat interactive, educational experience was added to the ship, they thought. A few weeks had passed before one of the employees, when walking through the same turret section, noticed something rather unusual about one of the plastic men. The head of the hand-made sailor, who was manning the gun, was ripped completely from its body. The humanoid shape remained upright while its head lay mysteriously by its feet.

"How unusual," exclaimed the first employee to the scene. No visitors were in the turret, or the adjacent areas during the time this crime was committed. To add to the unsettling factor, it would have taken an exhausting amount of strength to tear the head from its shoulders. No tools were used; no surveillance captured a culprit; a true mystery remained ... at least for a few more weeks. The head of the second human-shaped cutout was found apart from its body. Again, no one was to blame (staff or visitor). A cloud of disturbance and unease filled the air as employees realized the impossibility of anyone carrying out these acts. There were no sufficient explanations other than the unexplainable. The realm of the supernatural, maybe. But, why? Why would this poltergeist activity take place? Who is the target? What could be the intended message?

One Saturday morning, in the days when USS *North Carolina*

saw active duty, two sailors decided to take a shortcut to get to the breakfast area on time. The two young men raced through the ship's halls and scaled her various ladders and hatches; one hatch was chosen by the men through which to pass. This hatch was used to load torpedoes to the turret gun. There is a large spring that holds the tongue in place which locks torpedoes in the correct position. When activated, the spring sends this elongated piece of solid steel forward, thrusting it with speed similar to that of a bullet flying from the barrel of a gun. The rushing men failed to recall this spring and tongue duo. One by one, they climbed the ladder and dove through the hatch door.

The first man stood on the highest ladder rung. Throwing his arms in an upward motion, he leaped from the rung and through the hatch opening, catching and pulling himself successfully through the opening. Safely on the other side, it was now Tommy's turn. He too raced against time to reach the top of the ladder. Like his brother in arms, he swung his arms backwards then forwards to gain extra momentum. He flung his arms up and through the hatch opening while flicking his feet downwards.

When Tommy jumped, the loose spring which activated the tongue gave way. As the steel shot forward, the tongue and Tommy's head met in the center, cracking Tommy's skull. Unable to grab the ladder, he plummeted three levels to his untimely death. The first sailor watched Tommy in horror. Perhaps the dislocated heads belonging to the dummies is the ghost of Tommy reminding present generations of the terror which took place at turret number two.

Superficial mutilation is not the only path of communication utilized by the present ghosts. It is common practice for archivists to retrieve artifacts currently on display and, when safely transported to the collection space, perform artifact preservation/conservation as well as reviews. This is to ensure the longevity of each artifact, as well as make sure everything is accounted for. Such was the quest set before the archival team aboard battleship *North Carolina*. The professionals made their way to the area which was shared with turret number two. As you can see, many artifacts are displayed here. The archivists donned their white cotton gloves and prepared a museum-grade cart with anti-acid, archival-grade paper on which would rest the priceless objects.

One by one, they began to remove the nearly 100-year-old, war-related pieces from their display cases, placing them on the hard, gray, plastic cart, exposing them to the fresh air (or as fresh as air will get below the main deck). They systematically placed each object to ensure that they would not bump one another as an outcome of the vibrations created by the cart when its wheels are in motion. They also refused to stack the artifacts, as this is a fundamental rule when handling historic objects. After the team strategically unloaded the objects from their cases and nestled them, as if they were the most fragile of glasses, onto the librarian-styled cart, one archivist positioned herself by the handle bar, another by the hand placements opposite the first person, and one on each side of the cart, ready to stabilize any pieces at a moment's notice when the cart was in motion.

One began to push; the other pulled; and the two on each side glued their eyes to the surface of the cart as if their lives depended on it (which they did, in a way). The experienced group moved with effortless motions as the cart was transported with such ease, it appeared as if it were slightly levitating as it rolled. They reached the closed entrance way, their safety guard worked; no one entered the room while artifacts were in the open. The archivist closest to the large, dense door placed her gloved hands on the opening mechanism of the solid, movable barrier and turned it with great effort. Nothing happened. The door appeared to have a mind of its own... She made a second attempt, this time, executing more effort. Still nothing.

"Let me try," stated a second archivist in a confused tone. She was slightly larger, possibly stronger. She tried to properly activate the door's expertly designed mechanism. Surprisingly, her efforts were futile. One by one, each archivist tried their luck at escaping the room which had now turned into a holding cell. Confusion and feelings of claustrophobia set in as they realized that they had unknowingly traded their titles of "archivists" for roles as "hostages."

Here they remained, encapsulated, unable to scream for help. Who would hear them through the thickness of the battle-proof door?

Emotions grew. They knew who was at fault. They didn't know how to approach the culprit, however; they've never confronted a dead man before... "It must be the artifacts," stated one hostage. "I believe you're right," agreed another. She explained, "The door operated perfectly fine before our artifact handling commenced. Now, the door is sealed shut." The group seemed to share the same thought. From a level of cognitive functioning, it seems as if everyone was experiencing some level of hysteria but, according to the current, lived, experience, paranormal activity must be the case, they thought.

The team quickly retraced their steps. They unloaded the artifacts, this time, back into the display case, while all along keeping their ever-flawless standard of expertise. After reattaching the display case lid, they each removed the gloves and placed them on the cart. They advanced back to the seemingly welded-shut door. The smallest member of the hostage group reached the door first. She clamped her sweaty hands around the handle of the door and threw her hands, forcing the handle into the opening position. The door effortlessly opened. Each of the four professionals eagerly left that room, and the heavy weight of claustrophobic emotions within.

Farewell, Brave Soul

It is time to go now. I hope you have enjoyed this most terrifying tour. I offer a few last words of advice: to the men, do not tempt the unseen hands which linger—no, are kept captive—within the walls of the machine shop. They are the definition of fear. Women are welcome to wander the haunted decks of this ghost ship. I do warn, do not accidentally wander into the section known as "the Brig." An ever-increasing number of well-intentioned women report physical activity perpetrated by the spirits of the dishonorable men who were sent there.

Alas, these are mere warnings, simple guidelines, as it were. But you must prepare yourself, as you wander the stilled and (*sometimes*) hushed halls and rooms of this swaying war vessel, for the encounter with death—but not your own. The death of another who, though so quickly and untimely the kiss of death did happen upon him or her, still, somehow, wanders these very decks, waiting for you, *watching you*... Farewell, brave soul.

Index

Index